Discovering Literature Series

CHALLENGING LEVEL

The Lord of the Flies

A Teaching Guide

by Mary Elizabeth

Illustrations by Kathy Kifer

Community Strand

Dedicated to
Curt Crotty

GARLIC PRESS

Educational Materials for Teachers and Parents

899 South College Mall Road
Bloomington, IN 47401

www.garlicpress.com

Lord of the Flies
is available in many editions.
This study guide was prepared
using the following:

Lord of the Flies
Riverhead Books
The Berkley Publishing Group
200 Madison Avenue
New York, New York 10016

All page references in this guide are to the Berkley edition of *Lord of the Flies*.

ISBN 0-931993-96-2
Order Number GP-096

www.garlicpress.com

Table of Contents

NOTES TO THE TEACHER

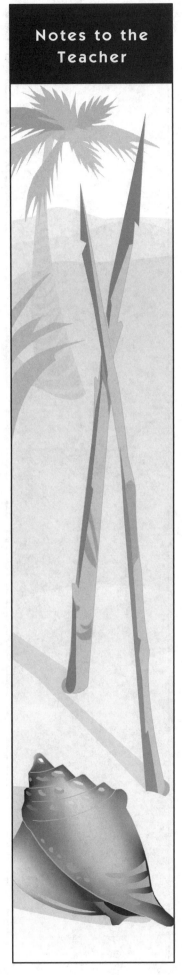

The Discovering Literature Series is designed to develop a student's appreciation for good literature and to improve reading comprehension. At the Challenging Level, we focus on a variety of reading strategies that can help students construct meaning from their experience with literature as well as make connections between their reading and the rest of their lives. The strategies reflect the demands of each literary selection. In this study guide, we will focus on beginning a book, setting and mood, plot, foreshadowing and flashback, characterization, forming hypotheses, point of view, rhetoric, irony, symbolism, rereading, theme, consulting outside references, and comparing and contrasting a book and a movie.

The following discussion explains the various elements that structure the series at the Challenging Level.

THE ORGANIZATION OF THIS LITERATURE GUIDE

Vocabulary

Since this book has relatively few vocabulary words, the **Chapter Vocabulary** for the entire book is introduced at the end of this introductory material. The words appear both in book-order (with page numbers from the Berkley edition) and in alphabetical order (again, with Berkley page numbers). You can display them on an overhead projector before each chapter is read, and guide students in using one of the vocabulary exercises listed below to preview the chapter vocabulary. Introducing the **Chapter Vocabulary** prior to students' reading insures that their reading is not disrupted by the frequent need to look up a word.

The **Chapter Vocabulary** includes definitions of key words from each chapter. To save time, students need only to copy, not look up, definitions. The more meaningful the vocabulary exercises are, the more easily students will retain vocabulary. Suggestions for teaching vocabulary include

1. Finding relationships between and among words helps students learn the words better than treating them separately. Have students create a web or other graphic, showing the relationships between and among the vocabulary words. Encourage them to add other related words to their web.
2. A group of words that is primarily nouns can be used to label a picture.
3. Have students use the words in a piece of writing, for example a poem, a one-act play, a diary entry written from the point of view of one of the characters.
4. Have students research the etymology of each word and keep notes on it.
5. Have students make and exchange crossword puzzles made with the vocabulary words.
6. Have students write and exchange a cloze exercise using the vocabulary words. A cloze exercise has a blank for each vocabulary word, and the surrounding context must clearly indicate which word belongs in each blank.

Because the vocabulary from all the chapters is presented together, you can also have students search for patterns of word use throughout the book to help them understand Golding's diction. For example, you might have them locate all the words throughout the book having to do with clothes, sound/speech, light/darkness, good/evil, adjectives describing behavior, etc.

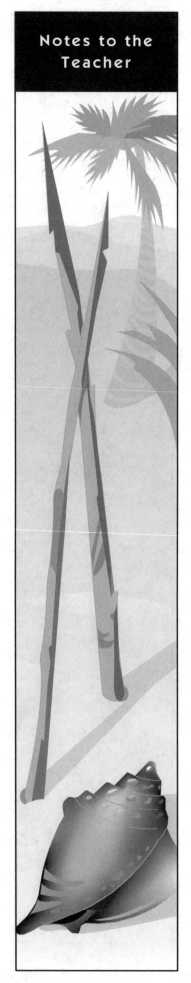

Chapter Pages

Each **Chapter Page** is organized into two basic elements: **Journal and Discussion Topics** and a **Chapter Summary.** One or more of the Journal and Discussion Topics can either be displayed on the board or on an overhead projector before each chapter is read. The selected Journal and Discussion Topics will help to focus the students' reading of the chapter. Choose questions that will not give away important plot elements.

• The **Journal and Discussion Topics** include questions for the students' **Reader Response Journals** and questions for **Discussion**. These topics will help students become engaged with the literature. Berkley page numbers are used to help locate references. An **Answer Key** is provided at the back of the book for each set of questions. Answers to complex questions are of necessity often incomplete and only suggestive. Students' answers should be more fully developed.

Students will benefit by reading with their journals beside them so they can easily note any unfamiliar vocabulary that was not presented to the class, questions they have about the literature, and their own reactions as they enter into the experience of the story. Journals can also be used for written dialogue between you and students. If you wish, periodically collect the journals and respond to students' comments. It is important for students to know beforehand whether their journals are private or public. In either case, journals should not be corrected or graded, but only recorded for being used. You may also wish to keep your own journal.

• **Discussion** can take place between partners, in small groups, or with the entire class participating. Students may also wish to reflect on the discussion by writing in their journals. Discussion starters include:

1. A group retelling of the chapter in which everyone participates.
2. Each group member telling
   a. the most striking moment in the chapter for him or her;
   b. a question she or he would like to ask the author or a character about the chapter; or
   c. what he or she liked most or least about the chapter.
3. A discussion of how the chapter relates to the rest of the book that preceded it.

Discussion can end with predictions about what will happen in the next chapter. Each student should note predictions in her or his journal.

Always ask students to retell (or summarize) the material. The retelling can be oral, artistic (for example, a storyboard), or prose. Retelling can take place in the discussion groups or in the journals.

• The **Chapter Summary** for each chapter is included for teacher use only. It provides an at-a-glance scan of the chapter events. Use it to refresh your memory about the contents of each chapter.

Groupings of Literature

We have among our titles a group of works that could be presented as part of a unit called "Community." We present groupings of literature so that you can easily group works as a unit. The works of literature in the "Community" unit resonate with each other, providing a multi-faceted look at a variety of **themes** such as:

- Government
- The Individual and the System
- Leadership
- Responsibility
- Freedom
- Choices
- Belonging
- Diversity and Unity
- Identity
- The Ideal Society

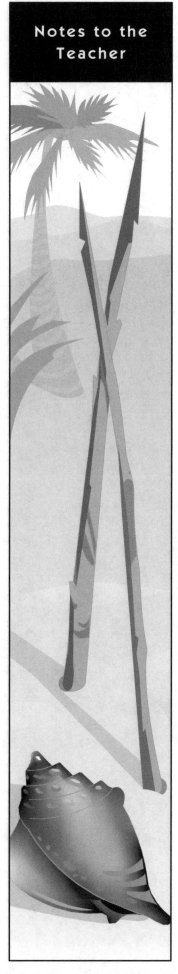

Since no substantial work of literature has only a single theme, "Community" is not the only possible grouping for these works of literature. But reference to themes can both help focus students' attention as they read and help link works of literature together in meaningful ways. In a similar way, a grouping of books can throw light on **Big Ideas**. Big Ideas worth considering include the following:

- What makes a community?
- How is our community important in our lives?
- How can we contribute to our community?
- How does the community context (cultural, social, etc.) affect individuals?
- How can individual and communal goals conflict or coexist?

Strategy Pages

Strategy Pages throughout the series have been developed to increase students' understanding of strategies they can use to enhance their understanding of literature. Some important examples are:

- Monitoring (such as adjusting reading rate; consulting outside sources for further information; using context, referring to illustrations to help clarify meaning; rereading; etc.)
- Identifying important information (such as marking a text)
- Summarizing
- Evaluating
- Understanding the tools that writers' use to make meaning—the elements of literature such as theme, plot, character, allusion, symbolism, metaphor, etc.

The pages for each literature selection reinforce the strategies important for engaging deeply with that particular work of literature. You may copy and distribute these pages. Students can answer on the back of the page or on a separate sheet of paper.

An Answer Key is provided at the back of the book for each Strategy Page. Answers to complex questions are of necessity incomplete and only suggestive. Students' answers should be more fully developed. Some Strategy Page questions require ongoing attention as the students continue reading.

Tests

At the end of each chapter grouping, a comprehensive open-book **Test** has been provided for your use. Each test includes vocabulary exercises and short essays. You may copy and distribute these pages.

An Answer Key is provided at the back of the book for each Test. Answers to essay questions are of necessity incomplete and only suggestive. Students' answers should be more fully developed.

Writer's Forum Pages

Suggestions for writing are presented under the **Writer's Forum** heading throughout this guide. You can choose from these suggestions or substitute your own creative-writing ideas.

Each Writer's Forum includes both instruction and directions for a particular writing task. Students will write in a variety of genres relating to the text and their own experience of the text. As you plan lessons, allow enough time for students to engage in the writing process:

- **Prewrite** (brainstorm and plan their work)
- **Draft** (give a shape to their ideas on paper)
- **Review** (revisit their work with an eye to improving it, on their own as well as with peers, with you, or with others)

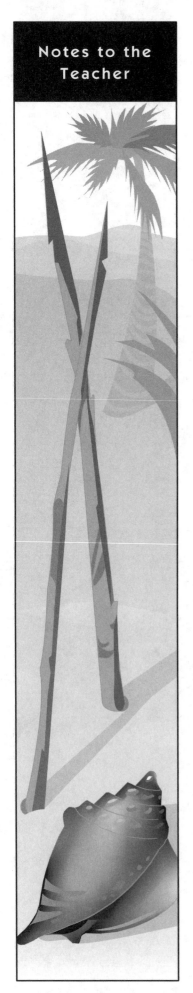

• **Revise** (make changes that they feel will improve their draft)
• **Proofread** (check for accuracy in grammar, mechanics, and spelling)
• **Publish** (present their work to others in some way)

An Answer Key is provided at the back of the book for each Writer's Forum. Answers are of necessity incomplete and only suggestive. Students' answers should be more fully developed.

History of Ideas Pages

One of the challenges of reading sophisticated works as a young adult is recognizing where the author's thought fits in the history of ideas. If the author is explicit, it can still require some research to understand where the author stands on particular issues. But it is especially difficult to place the book in an historical context when the ideas are implicit. Golding's book addresses ideas from the nature of humanity to the role of education. Certainly, *Lord of the Flies* can be, and is, read without explicit reference to Rousseau, et al. If you would like to address the history of the debate on some of the issues Golding brings up, you may wish to use these pages. They are grouped at the end of the book, but can be used before the students begin the book, as their individual topics become important in the narrative, or after students' reading is complete.

Theme Pages

This study guide offers two different ways to approach theme. One is the standard Theme Strategy Page (page 72) used in every work in this series. If, however, you would like to treat the themes in this work in more depth, there are pages at the end of the text that focus more deeply on some of the themes that Golding explores in the novel. (See Theme Pages, pages 78–85.) You may wish to use them while students read, introducing them as their individual topics become important in the narrative, or after students' reading is complete.

INTRODUCING THE LITERATURE

Students will be better prepared to become involved with the work of literature if they can place it in a context. The process of contextualizing a work of literature begins with accessing their **prior knowledge** about the book, the author, the genre, and the subject. A class discussion is a good forum for this to take place. After you have found out what, if any, familiarity students have with the book and author and what they have been able to discern about the genre and subject, you can provide any necessary background knowledge and, if it seems appropriate, correct any misapprehensions students have. (See **Strategy 1: Beginning a Book,** pages 16–17.)

Explain that in a work of fiction, an author creates an imaginary world. An important task in beginning a literature selection is to come to terms with that world. Point out that it is possible to consciously assess one's own understanding of literature and that this process is called **metacognitive reflection.** You may wish to model this process using a **think-aloud** approach as you go through the material on pages 16–17. To do this, simply read aloud the portions of *Lord of the Flies* needed to answer the questions, and speak aloud your thoughts as you formulate your responses, making explicit the connections and prior knowledge you are using in developing your thoughts.

After students have a beginning notion of the context of a work, you can proceed with the prereading activities that students will use prior to every chapter.

Sample Lesson Plan

Engaging **Prereading** activities include the following:
- Preview vocabulary and do a vocabulary exercise.
- Review the events of the previous chapter.
- Based on what you already know, examine your expectations about what will happen next, but be ready for surprises. Consider the chapter title and any illustrations. If you wish, you can use a prediction guide. Students can fill in the guide as a class, in groups, or individually.

During Reading students read with their Reader Response Journals. (You may wish to give them some of the journal and discussion topics before they read.)

Remind students of the questions that can help them to begin to understand a work of literature (see questions 1–6, page 17). You may wish to have students address these questions in their journals as they begin the book. Encourage students to continue using this kind of self-questioning in their Reader-Response Journals.

Additional journal activities they can use with every chapter include the following:
- A summary of the events of the chapter.
- Eevaluations of the characters and/or text
- Questions about what they have read
- Associations they have made between the text and other texts, experiences, or situations
- Notes on the images the text evoked
- Notes on the feelings the texts evoked

After Reading, students complete the Journal and Discussion Topics, the Writer's Forum and Strategy Pages, if any, and the Test.

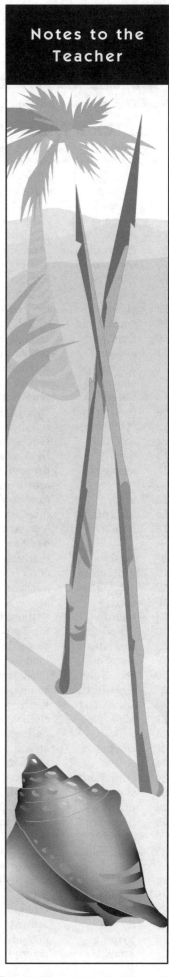

Notes to the Teacher

Vocabulary

Note: Page numbers are from the Berkley edition.

CHAPTER 1: THE SOUND OF THE SHELL

1	crooks	curves behind the knees
2	lodgments	resting places
3	proffer	offer
4	fledged	covered, as a bird with feathers
5	garter	a band worn to hold up a stocking
6	sidelong	sideways
7	motif	single or repeated design
7	efflorescence	blossoming
7	specious	deceptive
9	lolled	lounged
9	swathing	engulfing
10	effulgence	brilliance
10	enmity	ill-will
10	fronds	large leaves with many divisions
11	decorous	proper and in good taste
11	interposed	intruded; got between
12	embossed	raised
13	pursed	puckered
13	fluking	changing by chance
13	strident	harsh and loud
13	wubber	blubber; cry
15	fawn	light, grayish brown
15	jerseyed	dressed in jerseys (knitted garments like sweaters)
15	tow	/toe/ pale; straw-colored
15	incredulous	unbelieving; skeptical
16	hambone frill	a collar frill, resembling that put on baked ham
17	matins	morning prayer
17	precentor	choir leader
17	sniggers	snickers
19	furtive	sly
19	pallidly	without liveliness
19	chapter	for the cathedral
19	chorister	singer in the choir
19	clamor	loud din
20	obscurely	mysteriously
20	mortification	shame; humiliation
20	suffusion	flush
21	togs	clothes for a specific use
21	pallor	paleness
21	clouted	struck
21	crags	steep and rugged rocks
24	surmounted	topped
24	skewed	slanting
24	pliant	pliable; flexible
25	immured	walled in
25	communion	unity
25	under-dusk	darkness like dusk, but created by vegetation rather than by the waning light of day
26	defiles	gorges
27	bastion	stronghold
28	astern	toward the back of a ship
28	twining	meandering; curving
29	aromatic	fragrant
29	plonking	plunking (onomatopoeia)
29	traces	straps of a draft animal's harness (used metaphorically)
30	hiatus	break in time
30	enormity	great wickedness

CHAPTER 2: FIRE ON THE MOUNTAIN

35	induced	persuaded
36	confirmation	agreement
37	compelled	forced
39	swathes	areas similar to rows left by a mower
39	errant	disobedient
39	martyred	suffering
39	ebullience	exuberance; liveliness
41	officious	too eager to serve or advise
42	leeward	facing the same direction that the wind is blowing
42	windward	facing the direction from which the wind is coming
45	recrimination	an accusation made in retaliation
45	hayrick	large pile of hay
45	tumult	uproar
46	capering	playful leaping or dancing

CHAPTER 3: HUTS ON THE BEACH

50	festooned	decorated as with large loops of ribbon
50	tendril	slender, coiled, hanging plant structure
50	pendant	hanging
51	bolting	out of control
51	avidly	eagerly
51	inscrutable	not easily understood
52	castenet	percussion instrument clicked in the hand
52	seductive	tempting
52	vicissitudes	difficulties or hardships
52	contrite	sincerely sorry for shortcomings
53	gesticulated	gestured while speaking
54	compulsion	irresistible impulse or force
57	declivities	descending slopes
57	rapt	completely absorbed
58	tacit	unstated
61	susurration	murmur
61	sepals	modified leaves at the base of a flower's petals

CHAPTER 4: PAINTED FACES & LONG HAIR

62	whelming	engulfing, covering
62	opalescence	reflecting rainbow-colored light
62	impending	as though hanging suspended
62	blatant	noisy; clamorous
63	generic	without distinction; in general
64	belligerence	an aggressive, stubborn attitude
65	chastisement	punishment
65	impalpable	not capable of being felt
65	incursion	a breakthrough into enemy territory
65	detritus	debris
65	myriad	innumerable

66	runnels	little streams
66	crooning	singing softly
66	fibrous	with fibers or threadlike characteristics
67	swarthiness	darkness (of skin)
68	Samneric	"Sam and Eric" combined into a single name used indiscriminately for either twin
68	sinewy	strong
70	disinclination	mild preference for avoiding something
70	footling	useless
70	balm	a healing agent
72	ravenously	with greed
75	gouts	masses of fluid
75	lashings	(chiefly British) large amounts
78	malevolently	with hostility
78	gyration	revolving motion
80	ha'porth	contraction for *halfpenny worth*: a tiny amount
81	elemental	fundamental; resembling a great force of nature
82	nob	(chiefly British) one holding or having a superior position of respect or honor

CHAPTER 5: BEAST FROM WATER

85	apex	summit
85-6	reverence	respect; honor
87	tottery	unbalanced
92	expansively	with eagerness to expand on a topic
94	derisive	ridiculing
96	effigy	representation
96	lamentation	mourning out loud
97	indigo	deep reddish blue
98	sheered off	left the course
98	sod you	(chiefly British, vulgar) damn you
98	nuts	(vulgar) testicles
98	decorum	proper manners and good taste
98	inarticulate	unable to speak
101	tempestuously	like a tempest; stormily
101	bollocks	testicles
102	discursive	rambling
105	gibbering	babbling
105	incantation	formula of words with the power of a spell

CHAPTER 6: BEAST FROM AIR

108	waxy	in a rage
111	interminable	seemingly without end
111	tremulously	timidly
114	embroiled	involved in conflict
116	diffidently	with hesitation and respect
116	constrainedly	with restraint
118	chasms	deep clefts or gorges
118	polyp	invertebrate animals including jellyfish
118	leviathan	a great sea monster defeated by God in the Old Testament Book of Job
119	guano	excrement of sea birds
120	exulting	joyful
122	mutinously	rebelliously

CHAPTER 7: SHADOWS AND TALL TREES

123	dun	cheerless
123	coverts	thickets where animals can hide
124	scurfy	with a surface deposit
126	moors	(chiefly British) grasslands unusable for farmland; boggy areas
129	brandishing	waving about in a threatening manner
130	rugger	(chiefly British) slang for rugby
133	glowered	stared angrily
133	sagely	wisely
135	daunting	dismaying
137	windy	(slang; short for idiom "Got the wind up") nervous
137	infuriating	maddening
137	impervious	without feeling or response
138	bravado	foolhardiness

CHAPTER 8: GIFT FOR THE DARKNESS

144	prefect	student monitor in a private school
148	sanctity	holiness; inviolability
151	demure	modest
152	fervor	intensity
155	palled	grew uninteresting
155	paunched	with a potbelly
160	taboo	rule that makes something forbidden
160	demoniac	fiendish
160	smut	dirt
162	sufficiency	adequacy; enough

CHAPTER 9: A VIEW TO A DEATH

167	interspersed	interwoven; with something at intervals in between
168	corpulent	with a large, bulky body
168	looming	dark, indistinct, and deceptively large
171	derision	ridicule
171	succulent	juicy
171	sauntered	strolled
174	demented	insane
175	unendurable	not bearable
175	surged	rolled forward like a wave
176	furrowing	creating trenches in something
176	phosphorescence	ongoing emission of light

CHAPTER 10: THE SHELL AND THE GLASSES

179	befouled	made foul
184	torrid	scorching
184	assimilating	taking in and integrating
185	theological	relating to the study of God
190	barmy	(chiefly British) crazy
191	composite	something made up of distinct parts
193	purged	cleaned; freed
193	pills	(slang) testicles

Vocabulary, cont.

CHAPTER 11: CASTLE ROCK

195	luminous	glowing
195	myopia	near-sightedness
200	multitudinous	consisting of innumerable parts
200	propitiatingly	appeasingly; in order to regain favor
200	unquenchable	unstoppable
201	impenetrable	unable to be entered
201	pinnacles	peaks; spires
202	quavered	with a voice that trembled
204	ludicrous	ridiculous
205	sabers	curved swords
205	truculently	with aggressive savagery
206	cessation	stop
207	parried	warded off the blow
208	talisman	object considered to be a charm against evil
209	delirious	filled with a frenzied excitement

CHAPTER 12: CRY OF THE HUNTERS

217	inimical	hostile
218	antiphonal	responses alternating from one group to a second
218	ululation	howling
222	ensconce	conceal
222	cordon	a line of people set up to prevent passage through an area
222	diddle	fool
224	diaphragm	the separation between the chest and abdomen
225	elephantine	moving with clumsiness and intentness
226	crepitation	crackling
227	shied	started suddenly (past tense of *shy*)
231	obscurity	state of being unknown
232	drill	durable cotton twill fabric used for military uniforms
232	epaulettes	shoulder ornaments on a military uniform
233	distended	swollen from internal pressure

ALPHABETICAL WORDS

WORD	PAGE	MEANING
antiphonal	218	responses alternating from one group to a second
apex	85	summit
aromatic	29	fragrant
assimilating	184	taking in and integrating
astern	28	toward the back of a ship
avidly	51	eagerly
balm	70	a healing agent
barmy	190	(chiefly British) crazy
bastion	27	stronghold
befouled	179	made foul
belligerence	64	an aggressive, stubborn attitude
blatant	62	noisy; clamorous
bollocks	101	testicles
bolting	51	out of control
brandishing	129	waving about in a threatening manner
bravado	138	foolhardiness
capering	46	playful leaping or dancing
castenet	52	percussion instrument clicked in the hand
cessation	206	stop
chapter	19	for the cathedral
chasms	118	deep clefts or gorges
chastisement	65	punishment
chorister	19	singer in the choir
clamor	19	loud din
clouted	21	struck
communion	25	unity
compelled	37	forced
composite	191	something made up of distinct parts
compulsion	54	irresistible impulse or force
confirmation	36	agreement
constrainedly	116	with restraint
contrite	52	sincerely sorry for shortcomings
cordon	222	a line of people set up to prevent passage through an area
corpulent	168	with a large, bulky body
coverts	123	thickets where animals can hide
crags	21	steep and rugged rocks
crepitation	226	crackling
crooks	1	curves behind the knees
crooning	66	singing softly
daunting	135	dismaying
declivities	57	descending slopes
decorous	11	proper and in good taste
decorum	98	proper manners and good taste
defiles	26	gorges
delirious	209	filled with a frenzied excitement
demented	174	insane
demoniac	160	fiendish
demure	151	modest
derision	171	ridicule
derisive	94	ridiculing
detritus	65	debris
diaphragm	224	the separation between the chest and abdomen

diddle	222	fool
diffidently	116	with hesitation and respect
discursive	102	rambling
disinclination	70	mild preference for avoiding something
distended	233	swollen from internal pressure
drill	232	durable cotton twill fabric used for military uniforms
dun	123	cheerless
ebullience	39	exuberance; liveliness
effigy	96	representation
efflorescence	7	blossoming
effulgence	10	brilliance
elemental	81	fundamental; resembling a great force of nature
elephantine	225	moving with clumsiness and intentness
embossed	12	raised
embroiled	114	involved in conflict
enmity	10	ill-will
enormity	30	great wickedness
ensconce	222	conceal
epaulettes	232	shoulder ornaments on a military uniform
errant	39	disobedient
expansively	92	with eagerness to expand on a topic
exulting	120	joyful
fawn	15	light, grayish brown
fervor	152	intensity
festooned	50	decorated as with large loops of ribbon
fibrous	66	with fibers or threadlike characteristics
fledged	4	covered, as a bird is with feathers
fluking	13	changing by chance
footling	70	useless
fronds	10	large leaves with many divisions
furrowing	176	creating trenches in something
furtive	19	sly
garter	5	a band worn to hold up a stocking
generic	63	without distinction; in general
gesticulated	53	gestured while speaking
gibbering	105	babbling
glowered	133	stared angrily
gouts	75	masses of fluid
guano	119	excrement of sea birds
gyration	78	revolving motion
hambone frill	16	a collar frill, resembling that put on baked ham
ha'porth	80	contraction for *halfpenny worth*: a tiny amount
hayrick	45	large pile of hay
hiatus	30	break in time
immured	25	walled in
impalpable	65	not capable of being felt
impending	62	as though hanging suspended
impenetrable	201	unable to be entered
impervious	137	without feeling or response
inarticulate	98	unable to speak
incantation	105	formula of words with the power of a spell
incredulous	15	unbelieving; skeptical
incursion	65	a breakthrough into enemy territory
indigo	97	deep reddish blue

induced	35	persuaded
infuriating	137	maddening
inimical	217	hostile
inscrutable	51	not easily understood
interminable	111	seemingly without end
interposed	11	intruded; got between
interspersed	167	interwoven; with something at intervals in between
jerseyed	15	dressed in jerseys (knitted garments like sweaters)
lamentation	96	mourning out loud
lashings	75	(chiefly British) large amounts
leeward	42	facing the same direction that the wind is blowing
leviathan	118	a great sea monster defeated by God in the Old Testament Book of Job
lodgments	2	resting places
lolled	9	lounged
looming	168	dark, indistinct, and deceptively large
ludicrous	204	ridiculous
luminous	195	glowing
malevolently	78	with hostility
martyred	39	suffering
matins	17	morning prayer
moors	126	(chiefly British) grasslands unusable for farmland; boggy areas
mortification	20	shame; humiliation
motif	7	single or repeated design
multitudinous	200	consisting of innumerable parts
mutinously	122	rebelliously
myopia	195	near-sightedness
myriad	65	innumerable
nob	82	(chiefly British) one holding or having a superior position of respect or honor
nuts	98	(vulgar) testicles
obscurely	20	mysteriously
obscurity	231	state of being unknown
officious	41	too eager to serve or advise
opalescence	62	reflecting rainbow-colored light
palled	155	grew uninteresting
pallidly	19	without liveliness
pallor	21	paleness
parried	207	warded off the blow
paunched	155	with a potbelly
pendant	50	hanging
phosphorescence	176	ongoing emission of light
pills	193	(slang) testicles
pinnacles	201	peaks; spires
pliant	24	pliable; flexible
plonking	29	plunking (onomatopoeia)
polyp	118	invertebrate animals including jellyfish
precentor	17	choir leader
prefect	144	student monitor in a private school
proffer	3	offer
propitiatingly	200	appeasingly; in order to regain favor
purged	193	cleaned; freed
pursed	13	puckered

quavered	202	with a voice that trembled
rapt	57	completely absorbed
ravenously	72	with greed
recrimination	45	an accusation made in retaliation
reverence	85-6	respect; honor
rugger	130	(chiefly British) slang for rugby
runnels	66	little streams
sabers	205	curved swords
sagely	133	wisely
Samneric	68	"Sam and Eric" combined into a single name used indiscriminately for either twin
sanctity	148	holiness; inviolability
sauntered	171	strolled
scurfy	124	with a surface deposit
seductive	52	tempting
sepals	61	modified leaves at the base of a flower's petals
sheered off	98	left the course
shied	227	started suddenly (past tense of *shy*)
sidelong	6	sideways
sinewy	68	strong
skewed	24	slanting
smut	160	dirt
sniggers	17	snickers
sod you	98	(chiefly British, vulgar) damn you
specious	7	deceptive
strident	13	harsh and loud
succulent	171	juicy
sufficiency	162	adequacy; enough
suffusion	20	flush
surged	175	rolled forward like a wave
surmounted	24	topped
susurration	61	murmur
swarthiness	67	darkness (of skin)
swathes	39	areas similar to rows left by a mower
swathing	9	engulfing
taboo	160	rule that makes something forbidden
tacit	58	unstated
talisman	208	object considered to be a charm against evil
tempestuously	101	like a tempest; stormily
tendril	50	slender, coiled, hanging plant structure
theological	185	relating to the study of God
togs	21	clothes for a specific use
torrid	184	scorching
tottery	87	unbalanced
tow	15	/toe/ pale; straw-colored
traces	29	straps of a draft animal's harness (used metaphorically)
tremulously	111	timidly
truculently	205	with aggressive savagery
tumult	45	uproar
twining	28	meandering; curving
ululation	218	howling
under-dusk	25	darkness like dusk, but created by vegetation rather than by the waning light of day

unendurable	175	not bearable
unquenchable	200	unstoppable
vicissitudes	52	difficulties or hardships
waxy	108	in a rage
whelming	62	engulfing, covering
windward	42	facing the direction from which the wind is coming
windy	137	(slang; short for idiom "Got the wind up") nervous
wubber	13	blubber; cry

Bibliography

As you and your students immerse yourselves in this work of literature, you may wish to consult other works by the same author, thematically related works, video and/or audio productions of the work, and criticism. Here is a brief list of works that may be useful:

•WORKS OF LITERATURE

Adams, Richard	*Watership Down*
Ballantyne, R.M.	*The Coral Island*
Defoe, Daniel	*Robinson Crusoe*
Frank, Anne	*Diary of a Young Girl*
Huxley, Aldous	*Brave New World*
Lowry, Lois	*The Giver*
Orwell, George	*Animal Farm*
Orwell, George	*1984*
Pullman, Philip	*The Golden Compass*
Ransome, Arthur	*Swallows and Amazons*
Shakespeare, William	*Julius Caesar*
Shakespeare, William	*Romeo and Juliet*
Shakespeare, William	*The Tempest*
Stevenson, Robert Louis	*Treasure Island*
Vonnegut, Kurt	*Harrison Bergeron*
White, T.H.	*The Sword in the Stone*
Wyss, Johan	*Swiss Family Robinson*

•A FEW WORKS OF CRITICISM

Harold Bloom (ed.). *Lord of the Flies Modern Critical Interpretation*. 1992.

Thomas M. Coskren, O.P. "Is Golding Calvinistic?" *America*, CIX (7/6/63) pages 18-20.

L. L. Dickson. *The Modern Allegories of William Golding*. 1990.

Lawrence S. Friedman. *William Golding*. 1993.

Samuel Hynes. *William Golding*. 1964

Mark Kinkead-Weekes and Ian Gregor. *William Golding: A Critical Study*. 1968.

Patrick Reilly. *Lord of the Flies: Fathers and Sons: Twayne's Masterworks*. 1993.

David Spitz. "Power and Authority: An Interpretation of Golding's *Lord of the Flies*." *The Antioch Review*, Spring 1970, pages 21-33

•PERFORMANCES

If you want to experience *Lord of the Flies* in another media, this list will help you. I strongly urge you not to show videos or play audios until students have completed their reading.
VHS:

  Lord of the Flies. Peter Brook, 100 minutes. 1963.
  Lord of the Flies. Harry Hook, 90 minutes. 1990.

Audio cassettes:

  Lord of the Flies. Unabridged. Read by the author with his commentary: about 300 minutes.
    Listening Library, an imprint of the Random House Audio Publishing Group.

STRATEGY 1   Beginning a Book

An artist or craftworker about to create a work, chooses from a set of standard tools, techniques, and products. The composer, for example, can choose from a wide variety of styles of music: rap, Gregorian chant, jazz, ragtime, New Age, ethnic, classical, etc. The composer can prepare the piece for human voices, for orchestral or band instruments, for Renaissance instruments or ethnic ensembles, and complement this with sounds from nature, synthesizer or other electronic sounds, etc., in order to create an impression, set a mood, make a statement, or tell a story. The choreographer may borrow melodies from existing works and may incorporate other people's (or his or her own) words into the piece. The product may be an improvisation, a symphony, a song, a chant, etc. And the techniques used may include certain conventions, such as theme and variations, repetition, etc., which the composer may choose to employ or not. The composer cannot and does not use every technique and style in each piece, and each composer's choices are guided by his or her goal, which might be the answer to a question such as, "How can I effectively communicate my vision?" The listener hearing the music performed perceives it over time, and may not be able to take in the whole at once. There may or may not be an opportunity for a second hearing. Attending to detail, movement, rhythm, pattern, and the effect of the whole, the listener brings his or her past experience to bear and can come to understand the music in some meaningful way.

The writer is an artist who works in words that create images, thoughts, and feelings in the reader. Like the composer, the writer works to communicate a vision to people without speaking to them directly in conversation. The reader's understanding of the standard tools, techniques, products, and conventions of the writer helps the reader to comprehend the writer's vision. But at the same time that we try to understand the writer's communication, we must acknowledge that each reader also brings an individual and unique understanding to the act of reading, and so no two readers will experience a book in exactly the same way, just as no two listeners will have identical experiences of a piece of music. Different readers will have different insights and feelings, so discussion between and among readers can enrich the experience of all.

Beginning a book is particularly important, because readers starting a book are entering a new and uncharted territory. When you begin a book, paying particular attention to the writer's use of tools, techniques, and conventions can help.

TITLE: It is a convention for a novel to have a title, found on the front cover, the spine, and the title page. The title of the book may explicitly tell what the book is about, may hint about the story, or may seem very mysterious. Depending on the title, you may feel interested, curious, hopeful, etc. The author's name follows immediately after the title. If you know anything about the author already, for example, that Golding won the Pulitzer Prize in 1983, it might help you make predictions about the content of the book.

BOOK COVER: Most books have a picture on the cover. The writer may or may not have had a voice in what appears, so the illustration may not represent the writer's vision.

COPYRIGHT PAGE: The copyright page tells the dates of the book's publication. It can help you know whether the book is recent or older.

OTHER BOOKS BY: Sometimes there is a list that names other books by the same author. If you are familiar with any of these other works, you may have some idea of what is to come. This is also true if you have heard about the book from friends, read a book review, heard the book on audiotape, or seen a movie version. This is some of your prior knowledge about the book.

TABLE OF CONTENTS: While some books have unnamed divisions, sometimes authors title their chapters. Golding has done so, and the titles may provide hints to you about the plot of the book.

INSIDE ILLUSTRATIONS: Some books are illustrated throughout with drawings, paintings, photographs, etc. In most editions, this book is not.

BOOK COVER BLURBS: The notes on the back cover are advertising, meant to give away enough of the story to pique your interest and convince you to buy the book. The back blurb for the Berkley edition of *Lord of the Flies* has analysis which (in my opinion) you should skip because it gives away part of the plot and will interfere with your reading of the book.

FIRST FEW PARAGRAPHS: The first few paragraphs of the story provide the writer with the first opportunity to introduce the characters, plot, setting, and theme(s) of the story. Read carefully to learn as much as you can about the world of the book.

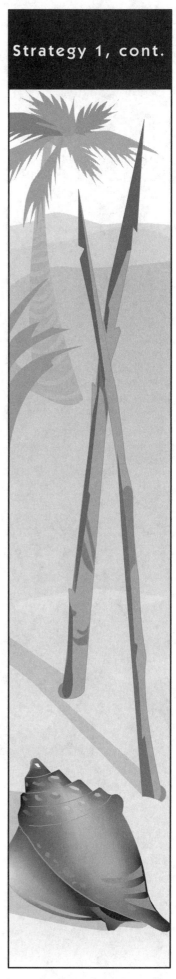

1. What is your reaction to the title of the book?
2. Based on the title, what do you think this book will be about?
3. Describe the jacket illustration. What can you gather from it?
4. How long has it been since this book was first published?
5. What, if anything, do you already know about Golding, his works, or *Lord of the Flies*?
6. What literary award has the author won? What does that signify to you?

Read to the line at which Ralph tells Piggy that he's going to get his clothes, and answer the following questions:

7. What do you think of Ralph? of Piggy?
8. What situation do Ralph and Piggy face?
9. What is the narrator like? Can you trust the narrator's perceptions? How did you decide?
10. Who seem(s) to be the most important character(s)? How can you tell?
11. Where does the story take place? Is it a real setting or a setting created by the author? What special characteristics does the setting have?
12. What clues are there to the genre of this story?
13. What does the focus of the story seem to be?
14. What do you predict will happen next in the story?
15. What more do you want to know about the setting and the characters?

Chapter 1 The Sound of the Shell

Journal and Discussion Topics

1. Describe the relationship between Piggy and Ralph.
2. Now that you've finished the first chapter, what do you think the story will be about? What evidence supports your conclusion? Have your ideas changed significantly? Explain.
3. Notice what Ralph, Jack, Roger, Simon, and Piggy do in their first actions. What impressions do their actions leave on you?
4. What unexpected or unusual uses of language do you notice in this chapter? What do you think is the purpose of each?
5. What is the community like so far?
6. What factors contribute to Ralph's election?
7. What does the incident with the piglet who escaped convey to you?
8. Do you think Ralph will be a successful leader? Explain.
9. What factions do you see forming among the group?

Summary

A group of schoolboys from England—some of whom were previously acquainted, but most of whom are strangers to each other—are being evacuated from a war zone when their plane is attacked and they are dropped onto an uninhabited island in the South Pacific. We first meet Ralph—a fair-haired, athletic twelve year old with an easy, carefree manner—and then Piggy—a fat, near-sighted boy who suffers from asthma, speaks in a lower-class dialect, and who has to excuse himself from his first conversation with Ralph because he has diarrhea from eating the fruit that grows on the island. Piggy, however, quickly proves his intelligence as he analyzes the situation and shares his conclusions with Ralph, giving Ralph the idea of blowing the conch to call the other kids to a meeting so they can get organized (and then giving Ralph credit for the idea), while Ralph is fantasizing about the pleasures of life on a coral island.

As Ralph winds the conch, children age six to about twelve begin to gather, already disrobing in an attempt to get comfortable in the heat. As Piggy moves among the boys, trying to collect names and count bodies, a group of seven cloaked boys with caps marches into view, under order of their leader, a tall red-headed boy. He is Jack Merridew, chapter chorister and head boy, and they are the choir: Maurice, Roger, Bill, Robert, Harold, Henry, and Simon (who promptly faints)—the one group of boys that already knows each other.

Jack is disappointed at not finding a man with a trumpet in charge. As Ralph and Piggy begin to explain what has been happening, Jack quickly gathers the group into unity by making fun of Piggy. When Ralph suggests they have a leader, Jack challenges Ralph for chief, but receives only the votes of the choir, with all other votes going to Ralph. Ralph graciously offers that Jack maintain control of the choir, who, it is decided, will be hunters.

Ralph and Jack decide to go scouting to find out if they're really on an island, and take Simon along. Piggy wants to come, but Jack makes clear his disapproval, and Ralph, too, abandons him. When Piggy confronts Ralph with revealing his school nickname of "Piggy" to the other boys after being asked not to, Ralph responds, "Better Piggy than Fatty."

The explorers determine that it IS an island, and on the way back to the group, they encounter a piglet trapped in the vines. Jack draws his knife, but is unable to bring himself to stab it. Embarrassed by his failure, he promises to kill the next pig. The narrator tells us, "Next time there would be no mercy."

STRATEGY 2 Plot—The Design of a Story

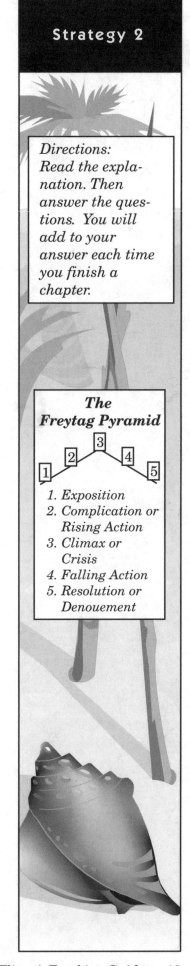

There are exciting stories and dull stories. There are westerns, adventure stories, mysteries, romances, thrillers, horror stories, science fiction stories, and fantasies. There are stories with happy endings and stories with sad endings. These differences can make stories seem worlds apart. But there are a common set of characteristics that almost all stories have—whether they are long or short, for adults or young people—that make them stories.

Every story has a plot or sequence of actions, a setting or settings where the action takes place, a character or group of characters who take action, and a narrator who tells the story to the reader.

People who study literature have come up with several different ways of talking about plot. When people talk about stories with young children, they often refer to the beginning, the middle, and the end. This is not just a notion for little kids. These three parts are the way screenwriters and television writers arrange their scripts. Dramatists, on the other hand, often work with a 5-act play. The 5 acts each represents an essential and sequential part of the drama. Narrative is also often presented in high school and college classes as having a 5-part structure as follows:

1. **Exposition**—introduction of essential background information, as well as characters, situations, and conflicts. Exposition may be found throughout a story, as well as at the beginning.

2. **Complication**—the beginning of the central conflict in the story.

3. **Crisis**—(sometimes called the **turning point**) usually the point at which the main character's action or choice determines the outcome of the conflict. Or, **Climax**: the high point of the action.

4. **Falling Action**—the time when all the pieces fall into place and the ending becomes inevitable.

5. **Resolution or Denouement**—the conflicts are resolved and the story is concluded.

The Freytag Pyramid

1. Exposition
2. Complication or Rising Action
3. Climax or Crisis
4. Falling Action
5. Resolution or Denouement

So do we look at a story as having 5 parts or 3 parts? One way we can think about it is to see where the 5 parts fit into the beginning, middle and end:

BEGINNING: Exposition

MIDDLE: Complication, ends with the Crisis or Climax

END: Falling Action (the beginning of the end) and Resolution

Writers adapt the plot structure to a particular story. They decide how much exposition should be included and where, how many conflicts there are, what's told to the reader explicitly, and what is left for the reader to figure out or deduce.

Sometimes a writer will introduce an unexpected character or force from outside the established story line to end the story. Such a device is called a *Deus ex Machina* from the appearance of a God (Deus) lowered from above by a machine (ex machina) at the end of some Greek tragedies. When the writer uses this kind of ending, the structure of the story may be radically different from what is described above because there may not be a discernible crisis because the main character's action or choice may not be the determining factor in bringing about the resolution.

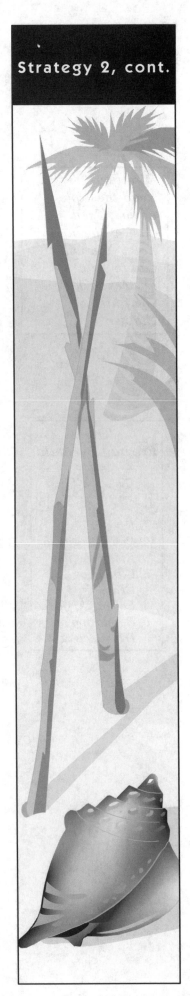

In some stories, the conclusion is purposely not conclusive on one or more levels. This may be done for a variety of reasons, including to reflect reality, which seldom comes in neat, tidy packages.

1. As you read *Lord of the Flies*, pause at the end of each chapter and identify for yourself where it fits in the plot structure. Place it on a Freytag Pyramid of your own. The shape of your pyramid may not exactly match the model in the margin.

STRATEGY 3   Forming Hypotheses

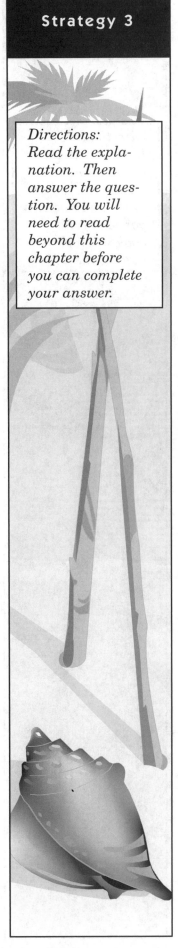

Sometimes we make guesses about causes, results, and intentions. When we guess, we may rely on intuition or what we wish to be true more than anything else. A **hypothesis** is special in that it is an *educated* guess. Unlike a "regular" guess, it is a prediction based on evidence.

Some people associate the word *hypothesis* strictly with scientific investigation. But that is not the limit of its application. Readers are constantly making and testing hypotheses about story characters' reasons for acting and making choices, about what will happen next in the plot, and about the author's intentions. Here are some criteria for a good hypothesis:

- **It should be of significance in the world of the story.** In some stories, for example, *The Iliad* by Homer, nature serves primarily as a portion of the setting—it is not invested with a lot of meaning. In *Lord of the Flies*, on the other hand, the descriptions of nature seem from the start to convey meaning. When the boys survey the island from the mountain, it seems wonderful to them, like a paradise. On the other hand, the "witchlike cry" and "skull-like coconuts" mentioned in the first few pages are both striking images that suggest evil. They are not descriptions that can be skipped over or ignored. The damage caused by the plane cabin is called a "scar," as if humankind's arrival on the island has "wounded" nature. It seems apparent that the author is carefully shaping the mood with the description of the island.

- **It should be clearly stated and specific so that you can easily tell what it means, but it should reach beyond what you know for certain.** If you formed a hypothesis, ***Maybe the description is important,*** it would not do you any good. That the description is significant is something we have already established. A hypothesis is a statement that you do not yet know the truth of.

- **It should identify the motivation, result, or intention that you think you have identified.** For example, some of the description of the island makes it seem like a paradise. The elements noted above, however, make it seem evil. Given the evidence, you might form the following hypothesis: ***Maybe the island is neither good nor evil, but equivocal.*** Once you form a hypothesis, you should look for further information to verify or disprove it.

1. Form a hypothesis about the role nature will play in the plot of *Lord of the Flies.*

   - Collect and record evidence from Chapter 1 that supports your hypothesis.
   - Now write your hypothesis and give the evidence that supports it. You may wish to arrange the evidence in the order of decreasing importance (most important point first) or increasing importance (most important point last).
   - Finally, as you continue reading, add a paragraph to your paper with a revision of your hypothesis based on new information and insights after finishing each chapter.

Directions: Read the explanation. Then answer the question. You will need to read beyond this chapter before you can complete your answer.

STRATEGY 4 — Characterization

A **character** in a story is someone or something whose actions, choices, thoughts, ideas, words, and/or influence are important in developing the plot. Characters are often people, but also include other living creatures, and sometimes even non-living things. A force, such as good or evil, can operate as a character in a story.

Most stories have a single character or a small group of characters whose goal or problem is the core of the plot. This character or group of characters is called the **protagonist**. The protagonist does not have to be good, but a good protagonist may be referred to as the "hero" of the story. Readers usually identify with the protagonist and hope that the protagonist will succeed in attaining his or her goal. The character, group, or force that opposes the protagonist is called the **antagonist**. In certain stories, this character may be referred to as the villain.

Characters, whether human or not, have what we call "personality"—a set of characteristic traits and features by which we recognize them. Personality is what helps us distinguish one boy on the island from another boy on the island, one eleven-year-old from another eleven-year-old.

Characterization is the name for the techniques a writer uses to reveal the personality of characters to the reader. Characterization is achieved in a number of different ways:

- **WORDS**—comments by the narrator, dialogue by others about the character, as well as the character's own words; what is said, as well as *how* it is said—dialect, slang, tone, are important
- **THOUGHTS**—what's going on in the character's mind, and the character's motives and choices
- **APPEARANCE**—the character's physical characteristics and clothing
- **ACTIONS**—what the character does
- **INTERACTIONS**—how the character relates to others
- **NAMES**—often symbolic of a major character trait or role
- **CHOSEN SETTINGS**—the items, furnishings, etc. that the character chooses to surround him- or herself with
- **CHANGE/DEVELOPMENT**—the occurrence of and direction of change or development a character undergoes inwardly

1. What is the first activity that Ralph engages in? Piggy? How does this make you think about each of them?

2. What is the effect on you of the dealings about Piggy's name?

3. How does Simon interact with the others?

4. How would you characterize Jack and his role in the story so far?

5. How does Ralph seem different in Jack's company than in Piggy's company?

6. How does the incident with the candle buds reveal differences among Jack's, Ralph's, and Simon's personalities?

Writer's Forum 1   Description

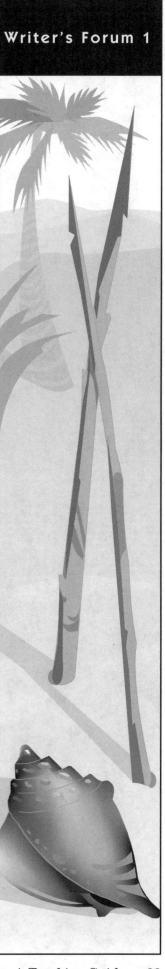

In a piece of descriptive writing, you let the readers know about the attributes of something so they can picture it in their mind's eye. You choose the features to mention based on what stands out among the physical properties and internal attributes of what you are describing, and these features will change depending on your topic. For example, if you were describing the forested part of the island, you might choose features such as "vegetation," and "noises." If, however, you were describing a character— Ralph, for example—you would use different features: physical appearance, personality traits, actions, and habits.

Here are some questions you can use to help you formulate your description of a place or object:

- What is it?
- What are its attributes?
- How is it apprehended by the senses—how does it look, smell, taste, feel, sound?
- How does it relate to other things in its environment or context?
- How can it be described by the 5 W's and How?

The way you organize the information in the description of a place or object can vary depending on what you are describing. Organization can help convey meaning. You can organize your description from

- top to bottom
- front to back
- side to side
- inside and outside
- around the perimeter
- from the beginning to the end of its cycle or process
- most important trait to least important (or vice versa)

When you are describing a person, you can organize using the elements that work together to create characterization:

- manner of verbal expression
- appearance
- interactions with others
- change/development
- thoughts, motives, choices, feelings
- actions
- meaning of name, if important or symbolic

Source words that can help you express concepts of continuity and diversity in your description of a person, place, or thing include the following:

- also
- and
- as well as
- similarly
- besides
- furthermore
- likewise
- alike
- in addition
- too
- at the same time
- resemble

- differ
- whereas
- however
- while
- but
- on the contrary
- conversely
- though
- on the other hand

1. Write a description of the beach on the island. Then write a description of Ralph, Jack, or Piggy. When you are done, write a brief reflection on the differences in content and organization between your two descriptions.

Chapter 2 Fire on the Mountain

Journal and Discussion Topics

1. What changes have taken place in the community in this chapter?
2. Describe the role Piggy takes in Ralph's government and in the community.
3. Do you believe that Ralph was going to say what Piggy said he was going to say (page 34)? Explain.
4. What do you think of Ralph's handling of the boy who told about the snake? Why do you think Ralph acted as he did?
5. What do you think the beast is?
6. What are the goals of this society? Are they reasonable? How do they go about achieving them?
7. How is Ralph's government working?
8. Describe the relationship of Jack and Ralph.
9. What episodes reveal a streak of violence in Jack?
10. What caused the out-of-control fire in your estimation?
11. What do you think happened to the small boy with a "mark on his face"?

Summary

The three explorers—Ralph, Jack, and Simon—return, and Ralph blows the conch to call a meeting. The group learns from Ralph that they are on an island; that pigs give the possibility of eating meat; and that there are no grown-ups, meaning, he says, that they will have to take care of themselves. Ralph begins to introduce some rules of order to the undisciplined group (such as the person holding the conch has the floor), when Piggy interrupts and stubbornly introduces a note of reality by leading the others to see that no one knows where they are. Ralph, claiming that he was about to say that, begins an idealistic description of the "good island" and the boys' ideas of what life will be like is shaped by the fiction they have read: *Treasure Island, Swallows and Amazons,* and *Coral Island.*

A second note of unrest is introduced by one of the six-year olds, distinguished in the text only by the mulberry-colored birthmark on his face. Supported by Piggy, while the others make fun of him, he asks about a "snake-thing" or "beastie"—a big one that comes out in the woods when it's dark. Ralph declares over and over that there isn't a beastie, that they don't live on islands this size, that the boy must have had a nightmare, and when these things don't comfort or stop his talk of the snake-thing, Ralph finally yells at him, "But I tell you there isn't a beast!" bringing the assembly to silence.

The idea of a beast dismissed, Ralph turns back to his goals: to have fun and be rescued, which he claims is certain to happen, using specious reasoning which none of the boys recognizes as such. He then proposes to assist rescue efforts by maintaining a fire on top of the mountain so that passing ships might spot the smoke. The boys take up the cry of "fire," and Jack yells "follow me" and takes off. Ralph's calls for quiet are ignored, as the entire group, save Ralph and Piggy, take off up the mountain—and Ralph follows shortly afterwards. Piggy, disgusted, collects the conch and follows.

Jack engages the choir in building a pile, and soon everyone but Piggy is working in a spirit of camaraderie and merriment until Jack and Ralph discover simultaneously that they have no way to light the fire. Jack realizes they can make a fire by focusing the sun with Piggy's spectacles and snatches them off his face, throwing Piggy into a panic since he can barely see without them.

Ralph starts the fire and yells for the others to get more wood, but the wind on one side of the mountain picks up and soon the pile is cinders. Piggy points out the uselessness of the fire, but Jack yells at him to shut up, and Ralph changes the subject to a discussion of a fire crew and the need for rules, the first being that where the conch is there is a meeting. Jack, who a minute before had said the conch had no power on the mountain top, agrees with Ralph and emphasizes the need for rules, pointing out that they are English, not savages.

As they plan the fire crew and lookouts, Roger, who has been watching the sea without seeing a ship, suggests that perhaps they won't be rescued. Ralph is reiterating that they will be rescued, when Piggy takes the conch and interrupts, again criticizing the lack of planning that went into the fire and the prejudice with which he is treated, when suddenly he sees that the fire has not completely died—the boys have inadvertently set half the mountain on fire. But soon all the boys except Piggy are giggling, and he furiously points out that they need shelters more than anything, but they're not putting first things first. He blames the group, rather than Ralph, saying that by acting so quickly they don't give Ralph time to think, and by acting so unthinkingly they are jeopardizing essentials, like their food supply. And lastly, he directs their attention to the most terrifying consequence: they don't know how many little kids there were, and at least one, the little boy with the mulberry-colored birthmark, is missing. Gasping for breath as his asthma comes on, Piggy asks repeatedly, "where is he now?" And Ralph replies, "Perhaps he went back to the, the,—"

STRATEGY 5

References and Allusions— A Story with a Past

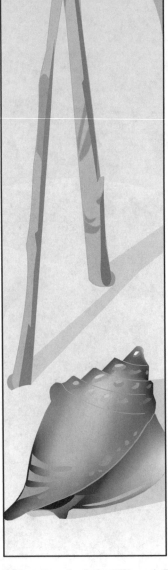

A **reference** is a mention of something outside the work you are currently reading. It could be a reference to a real or imaginary event, person, or place; or another literary work (often in a quotation), an aspect of culture, or a fact. References are often documented.

An **allusion** is an *indirect* reference—one that you need to recognize as a reference without the author telling you that it is one. After you recognize the allusion, you need to figure out what it means in the context. Sometimes an author will include clues like quotation marks, or introductory words (as the great philosopher once said . . .), or use a name. But sometimes, especially if recognizing and understanding it are not essential to the author's point or if the author assumes that virtually every reader will recognize the allusion, the author may not signal the allusion. S/he may, instead, rely on readers sharing a common knowledge of literature, history, biography, science, and art that in most cases will help readers figure out meanings. Sometimes allusions can be like private jokes, inserted for those who can get them. Allusions help the reader see the work as part of a greater literary tradition.

Many references and allusions support or reinforce the meaning in the text. But this is not their only possible purpose. References and allusions can provide contrasts as well as parallels.

THE CORAL ISLAND

The first allusion in the story would have been pretty obvious to British boys reading the book when it first came out, but is not at all obvious to us reading the book now. It occurs in the first chapter after Ralph gets dressed again and sits on a fallen trunk. The narrator observes, "Here was a coral island." This means nothing to most of us. Later, in Chapter 2, we read Ralph's claim, "While we're waiting we can have a good time on this island . . . . It's like in a book." And the response: *"Treasure Island—," "Swallows and Amazons—," "Coral Island,"* coupled with our knowledge of literature may lead us to recognize the first of these references as a book about an adventure on a deserted island, and to surmise that the other two references are titles as well. In addition, the words "coral island" may provide a vague echo back to those words in Chapter 1. Ralph continues "This is our island. It's a good island," and this is the tenor of the books to which the boys refer. These three books—*Treasure Island* by Robert Louis Stevenson, *The Coral Island* by R. M. Ballantyne, and *Swallows and Amazons* by Arthur Ransome—were popular reading for schoolboys when Golding wrote. Some background on *The Coral Island* will help you see why this passage is very important in the work as a whole.

Robert Michael Ballantyne (1825-1894), born in Edinburgh, Scotland, began writing children's books in 1856. His third book, *The Coral Island,* was published in 1857 and has never been out of print. Castaway stories were popular at that time. *The Swiss Family Robinson*, (1812–1813) is an example of such a story, portraying a family living in unity and peace after being shipwrecked on a South Sea island. What made *The Coral Island* unique was that Ballantyne was one of the first authors to tell of adventures in which there were no adults in which young men were adventurers and heroes.

The Coral Island is the story of three teenagers: Ralph—the narrator, Jack, and Peterkin. They are among a larger group that boarded ship from

England. Thrown overboard in a shipwreck, the three boys find themselves together on a coral island in the South Seas with no adults from their own society. Here, they convert a pirate, help a native "heathen" to marry the Christian chief whom she loves, and see the "savages" burn their idols and embrace the Gospel, after which they leave to sail home. If it is mentioned that in the New Testament, Peter the Apostle is also called "Simon," it may help you see that there are some immediate parallels between *Lord of the Flies* and *The Coral Island*—the names of three major characters and the unexpected landing of young men from Britain with no adults on an island in the South Seas. This description should give you an indication of the boys' expectations for their island experience in *Lord of the Flies*.

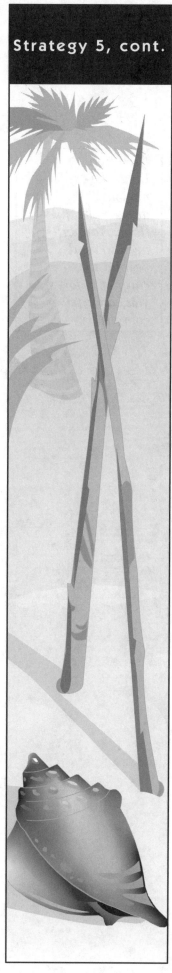

1. How do you think *Lord of the Flies* will differ from *The Coral Island*? Explain why you think as you do.

PARADISE

Another allusion that not every reader may recognize comes out through the references to snakes. It probably did not escape you that the little boy with the mulberry-colored birthmark claimed to see a snake/beast. But did you notice that Ralph brought a snake onto the island? When he undressed to go swimming in Chapter 1, the narrator says "He undid the snake-clasp of his belt." Whether or not there is an animal on the island that is a snakelike beast, the fear of a beast, and the true origins of this fear are important considerations, and Golding points to their importance by his choice of snake as opposed to any other animal. Snakes are an important literary symbol, and in the Western tradition, the germinal story is the story of Creation in the Book of Genesis (Chapter 3) in the Hebrew Scriptures or Old Testament of the Bible. In that biblical story of the beginnings of the human race, the snake is instrumental in what is called "the Fall" or "Original Sin." (See History of Ideas—Human Nature, page 75.)

2. Keep a record of the references to snakes and beasts. For each occasion, note where the mention occurs and who makes it. When you think you understand what Golding means by "the beast," write an explanation of what the beast represents.

STRATEGY 6   Plot—Conflict

*Directions:
Read the explanation. Then answer the questions. You will need to read beyond this chapter before you can answer completely.*

Conflict is the core of a story's plot. Conflict is what makes us wonder if the protagonist will attain his or her goal. Conflict is what adds suspense and excitement to stories. Usually there is one overarching conflict that takes up much of the book. But each chapter or scene in the book usually also has conflict on a smaller scale.

The struggles that a protagonist undergoes in a story can be either **internal** or **external**. In an **internal** conflict, the protagonist undergoes an interior struggle. He or she might have conflicting desires, values, personality traits, and/or motives. People often have internal conflicts as they grow and develop from one stage in their lives to the next. An internal conflict takes place within the character's mind and heart.

In an **external** conflict, the protagonist struggles with something or someone outside of himself or herself. The conflict may be with another individual, with a task or problem, with society, with nature, with an idea, or with a force, such as good or evil.

1. What does the overarching conflict in this story seem to be? Cite evidence to support your conclusion.

2. Make and fill in a chart like the sample below to show the main conflict for each chapter.

CHAPTER	CONFLICT
1	
2	
3	
4	
5	
6	
7	
8	
9	
10	
11	
12	

Writer's Forum 2

Journal

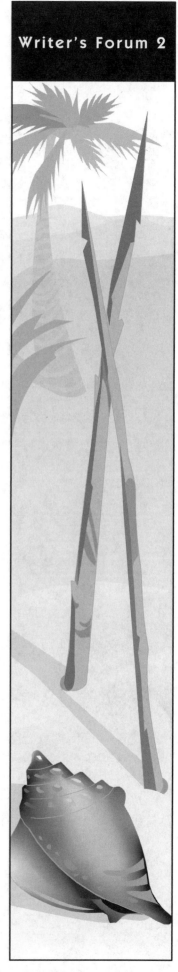

In a journal entry, you record the important events of the day from your own point of view. Journals may also contain memories, linking the present to the past. They sometimes include hopes, dreams, or plans for the future.

Some parts of a journal might be rather objective—for example, straightforward descriptions of people, places, or occurrences. Other parts might be very personal and subjective. Journal writing is often informal—because people usually write journals for themselves, they don't always follow all the rules of grammar, punctuation, and usage. People may use words with private meanings, abbreviations, slang, etc.

Journals are not necessarily all your own words. Some people choose to add quotations of others' words that they find helpful, interesting, or meaningful. Some people have a combination journal and scrapbook. Others draw in their journals. Since a journal is personal, it can take many forms.

1. Choose a character from this book. Suppose that in one of his pockets he has a small pad of paper and a pen or pencil. Write four journal entries for that character. You may wish to write one for each of four chapters (in which case, you will not be able to finish your writing until after Chapter 4), or find four occasions in Chapters 1 and 2. Feel free to embellish and elaborate the text, while staying "in character."

Chapter 3

Huts on the Beach

Journal and Discussion Topics

1. What indications of the passage of time does Golding give?
2. What signs are there of order and organization? What signs are there of disorder and failure?
3. How have the groups' goals changed?
4. What do you think of Simon? What is he doing at the end of the chapter?
5. How have attitudes toward the beast changed since Chapter 2?
6. Do you think Jack and Ralph will overcome their feeling of being separate and unable to communicate? Explain your thinking.
7. What do you think the next major plot development will be? What leads you to this conclusion?

Summary

We follow Jack as he stalks a pig, his eyes described as "nearly mad." He misses a spear shot and comes out of the forest to where Ralph and Simon are working on one of two shaky-looking shelters. Ralph complains about the lack of help, and Jack defends the choirs' dedication to getting meat, but Ralph keeps going until they are openly in disagreement, Ralph belligerently repeating himself and Jack shouting in rage. The argument quells somewhat when Ralph turns the conversation to why shelters are so needed—the littluns are afraid in the night. Simon captures the feeling when he says it's as if the littluns don't accept that it's a good island and as if they think the beastie is real. Recalling their joint discovery of being on a "good island" when they first met, Jack and Ralph come back into friendship for a few moments, only to have their argument erupt again shortly afterwards.

They both give up their tasks and go to the bathing pool, while the narrator turns to follow Simon. The narrator clarifies the misimpression Ralph has of Simon as a gay and wicked boy. Simon goes away from the group to a lonely, secret place, shielded from view by a screen of leaves. It is not clear what he is doing there.

STRATEGY 7

Rhetoric

Rhetoric means either the art of persuasion or the techniques used by writers in their craft. It includes considerations of sentence structure such as **parallelism** (the repetition of grammatical structures), for example in the description of the children coming out of the jungle in response to Ralph's first blows on the conch:

> "Some . . . more or less dressed, in school uniforms, grey, blue, fawn, jacketed, or jerseyed. There were badges, mottoes even, stripes of color in stockings and pullovers. Their heads clustered above the trunks in the green shade; heads brown, fair, black, chestnut, sandy, mouse-colored; heads muttering, whispering, heads full of eyes that watched Ralph and speculated." (page 15, Berkley edition)

Notice the repeated lists, separated by commas, to indicate the diversity of appearance among the children, although they are not yet identified to the reader by name or character.

Rhetoric also includes the techniques called "rhetorical figures" or "figures of speech." The rhetorical figures include the following:

- **simile** a comparison using words such as *like*, *as*, or *as if*.
  "The two boys . . . flung themselves down and lay grinning and panting at Ralph *like dogs*." (page 15, Berkley edition)

- **metaphor** a comparison in which two things which are in fact different are equated "The bat was the child's shadow...." (page 15)

- **personification** attributing human characteristics to non-human (often inanimate) things. Sometimes the qualities of something living but not human are applied to something inanimate for a related effect: "The flames, as though they were a kind of wild life, crept as a jaguar creeps on its belly toward a line of birch-like saplings . . . ." (page 45)

Sometimes its hard to tell if the attribution is personification or just animating the inanimate:

> "The heart of flame leapt nimbly across the gap between the trees and then went swinging and flaring along the whole row of them." (page 46)

- **onomatopoeia** the use of words that echo the meaning they represent
  ". . . plonking with weary feet on a track" (page 29)

Other rhetorical devices include **idioms**, expressions for which the meaning can't easily be figured out from the words themselves.

"You can't half swim." (page 8) means "You CAN swim really well," as if to say, "you don't do things by halves—you do them entirely well."

1. Find five similes and write them with their page numbers from the edition you are using.

2. Find five metaphors and write them with their page numbers.

Directions: Read the explanation. Then answer the questions. Some may require that you read beyond this chapter before you can answer. Some require reflection on your own experience and knowledge.

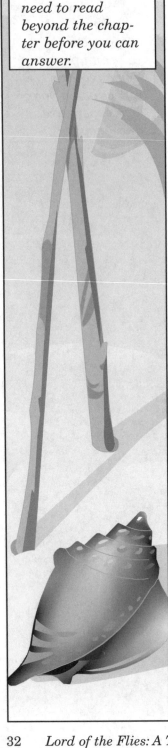

Strategy 8

Directions:
Read the explanation. Then answer the question. You will need to read beyond the chapter before you can answer.

STRATEGY 8   Irony

Irony comes from a Greek word meaning "someone who hides under a false appearance." When irony is used, things appear different, even the opposite, of what they really are: unexpected events happen, what people say is not what they mean. Authors use irony to create interest, surprise, or an understanding with their readers that the characters do not share. There are three types of irony.

Verbal irony is irony in the use of language. Verbal irony means that what is said is different from or the opposite of what is meant. A difference between tone of voice and the content of what is said is one kind of verbal irony. Understatement is another type of verbal irony. When Piggy says, "You got your small fire all right," on page 45 of the novel, and then we learn that fire is rushing uncontrolled down the side of the mountain, the statement is revealed to be a dramatic understatement, and very ironic.

In **dramatic irony**, there is knowledge that the narrator makes available to the reader, but the characters are unaware of it. In this story, Golding uses foreshadowing—hints in the text that suggest things to the readers without saying them directly—as one means of creating dramatic irony. (See Strategy 12—Foreshadowing and Flashback, page 50.)

Situational irony can occur either from the point of view of a character or the reader. It describes a situation when something that is expected with a great deal of certainty doesn't happen (this can be from either point of view) or when something that is intended fails to materialize (this is only possible from a character's point of view, except in Choose-Your-Own Adventures or other books in which the reader participates by making a choice). It is ironic that after everyone agrees at the meetings on the need to build shelters, nobody except Ralph and Simon actually do any great amount of work on the shelters (page 53 of the novel).

1. Keep a record of other examples of irony in this story as you continue to read.

Writer's Forum 3

List of Rules

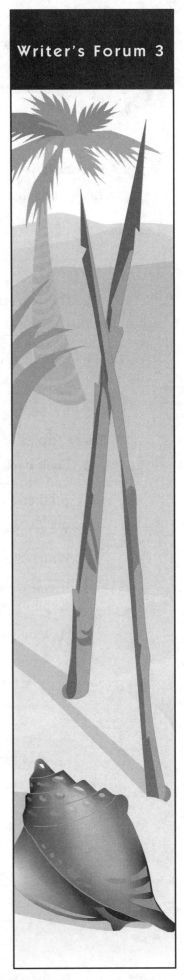

Rules are a set of guidelines that people agree to share or are forced to follow. Some rules may be explicit, while others may be implicit—agreed on without being publicly debated and defined. Sets of rules may include an explanation of the consequences for failure to observe the rules, as well as listing exemptions and exceptions. Usually, rules only work if they are clear, workable, and accepted by the community for which they were made.

Rules often begin with words like the following:

- Do
- Always
- Every
- If

- Don't
- Never
- Whenever
- No

1. Make a list of the rules, explicit and unspoken, that seem to govern the society on the island as of the end of Chapter 3. After each succeeding chapter, note new rules and changes to the rules. Explain why the changes take place.

Vocabulary

Look at each group of words. Tell why it is important in the story.

1. hambone frill, matins, precentor, chapter, chorister _____

   _____

2. fluking, strident, wubber _____

   _____

3. mortification, suffusion _____

   _____

Essay Topics

1. Look back at the predictions you made about the book for Strategy 1. Record what you think of your earlier predictions based on what you know now. Make new predictions for the rest of the book.

2. What's your favorite moment in the story so far? Explain your choice.

3. Which character do you think is the most interesting so far? Why?

4. If you were in the situation presented in this novel, what would your priorities be? Explain your thinking.

5. How do you think the relationships between the boys will develop over time?

Chapter 4

Painted Faces and Long Hair

Journal and Discussion Topics

1. What does it mean to have a "life so full that hope was not necessary and therefore forgotten"?
2. What factions now exist in the group?
3. What do you conclude about Roger from the way he teased Henry?
4. What effect did the painted "mask" have on the wearer? On others?
5. Piggy suggests making a sundial. Would a clock be useful? Explain your thinking.
6. In the crisis of the fire going out, Ralph uses language in several ways that haven't appeared in the book earlier. What are they and what does their use signify?
7. What does the analogy to a situation in church when Simon shushes Piggy (page 74) convey to you?
8. How do you feel about the boys' reaction to killing the pig?
9. From the narrator's description (page 77) do you think Ralph's or Jack's world is more appealing to the other boys? Explain.
10. What do you think this means: "Passions beat about Simon on the mountain top with awful wings." (page 78)?
11. Do you think Jack's apology was generous (as Jack thought) or a "verbal trick" as Ralph thought? Explain your thinking.
12. What was Simon ashamed of (page 80)?
13. What are the occurrences in this chapter that alienate Jack?

Summary

The boys slowly develop a rhythm of life, with the littluns having a separate existence from the bigger boys, an existence filled with fruit, chronic diarrhea, night terrors, and play, and occasional interruptions when the conch calls them. The littlun named Percival has a particularly difficult time, crying often, and is thought by the others to be crazy. The narrator describes a sequence in which first Roger and Maurice and then Roger alone purposely torment some of the littluns, including Percival. When these older boys leave, a littlun, imitating the big boys' behavior, throws sand in Percival's eyes, while another littlun throws sand at an imaginary Percival. Jack interrupts Roger's torment of the littlun called Henry to show him his new hunting strategy: painting his face with red and white clay to make himself less visible to the pigs, like soldiers using camouflage in war. The mask excites him, freeing him from "shame and self-consciousness," and compelling the others to do his bidding.

In the meantime, Ralph, Piggy, and Simon are relaxing, when Piggy suggests making a clock, an idea that Ralph immediately dismisses as impractical as he teases an unaware Piggy for his own amusement, while Piggy, seeing him smile, thinks that Ralph, unlike the others, really likes him. Suddenly Ralph is on his feet, yelling "Smoke!" because he's spotted a ship, but it slowly becomes apparent that there is no smoke showing from their signal fire. At this realization, Ralph tears off up the mountain, and on the way, after swearing at first, he becomes the first boy in the book to utter the name of God in a kind of abbreviated prayer. Simon and Piggy follow after him and find at the top a dead fire. The choir, whose job it was to tend the fire, has let it go out, just at the crucial time, and just as this realization strikes, the choir comes marching up the mountain with the pig they've just killed, the first meat the boys will have had since they landed. They are chanting, "Kill the pig. Cut her throat. Spill her blood."

The hunters, interrupting each other, begin telling the story of the hunt, while Ralph stands stock still and says, when he can get a word in, nothing but, "You let the fire go out." Jack is uneasy at this, and after a half-hearted explanation of the need for the fire crew to join in the hunt, returns to trying to convey the ecstasy of death and blood. Ralph finally tells the hunters that there was a ship and that because the fire went out, they have lost a chance to go home. Jack and Ralph face each other, representing "the brilliant world of hunting, tactics, fierce exhilaration, skill; and . . . the world of longing and baffled commonsense." Ralph argues that the fire was of first importance, and Jack claims that the group needs meat, hacking at the pig carcass as he argues.

When Piggy takes up Ralph's argument, Jack feels no more need to control himself, and socks Piggy in the stomach, then hits him in the head, causing Piggy's glasses to fall to the rocks. One of the lenses breaks. Piggy is now seriously disabled, being able to see with only one eye, but the seriousness of what this means to him is lost on the other boys as Jack's parody of Piggy's whiny complaint causes the hunters to laugh. Ralph almost joins in despite himself, but he controls himself and tells Jack, "that was a dirty trick." At this, Jack apologizes—for letting the fire go out, not for breaking Piggy's glasses—which he considers to be a great and generous gesture. Ralph considers this a mere verbal trick and refuses to say that he forgives Jack, only voicing the command, "Light the fire." But when the fire is built and Jack obviously has no means to light it without Piggy's glasses, it is Ralph who goes to Piggy and takes the spectacles from him without asking.

They cook the pig over the fire, and Jack asserts his power by not giving any to Piggy and then, when Simon gives his piece to Piggy, throwing meat at Simon's feet and commanding him to eat. After a period of silence, Maurice asks where the pig was found, and the story of the hunt is told more coherently than earlier. Then Maurice pretends to be the pig, and the hunters reenact the hunt, pretending to beat him and chanting the death chant, "Kill the pig. Cut her throat. Bash her in." They are interrupted by Ralph's announcement that he is calling an assembly immediately as he heads off down the mountain.

STRATEGY 9   Point of View

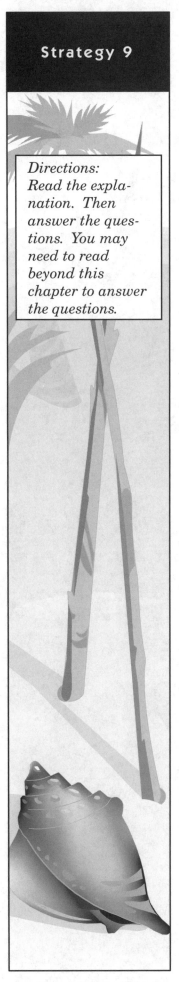

A story is always told by someone. This person is called the narrator. The narrator may be someone who participates in the action of the story, or someone outside the action of the story. The narrator may have a limited range of knowledge, or may know everything there is to know about the story. The narrator may be reliable or unreliable. All of these factors go into what is called the story's **point of view**.

Stories can be told in the **first-person point of view**. In this case, the narrator is usually someone who was present or involved in the action of the story, and this person tells the story using the pronoun *I* to indicate personal involvement.

Stories can also be told in the **second-person point of view**, which is distinguished by the fact that the narrator speaks to the reader as *you*, and addresses the reader directly, as if they were speaking together.

The **third-person point of view** is the point of view of a narrator who is separate from the action and tells it from a greater distance than a first-person narrator would.

A third-person narrator can be **omniscient**, knowing all the action of the story even including what is going on in all the character's minds and knowing what will happen in the end before it happens, or **limited** to knowledge of only the perspective of one character. When an author chooses a limited point of view, she or he is more likely to use devices like irony to allow readers to know more than the character from whose point of view the story is told.

It is an essential point that the reader cannot assume that the narrator of a story is the author. Usually the narrator of a work of fiction is a persona created by the author for the purpose of conveying the story. Thus, when quoting from this book, we should not say or write, Golding says, "Piggy was a bore" (page 70) a) because it is the narrator, not Golding, who says it and b) because at this point the narrator seems to be recording Ralph's thoughts, not the thoughts of the persona of narrator, let alone the thoughts of Golding.

1. Find three passages (besides the one from page 70 mentioned above) that show the narrator's access to Ralph's inner thoughts and feelings.

2. Does the narrator report anyone else's inner thoughts and feelings? Give examples.

3. What seems to be the narrator's relationship to the events of the story?

4. From what point of view is this story told?

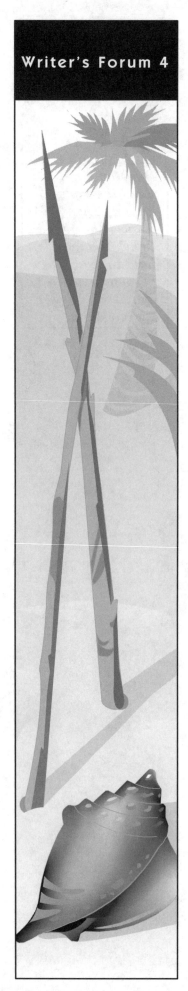

Writer's Forum 4 — Dialogue

Dialogue is a particularly powerful way to reveal a character's personality, thoughts, taste, and culture. The language that a character uses should reflect such important characteristics as age, education, and background. The level of formality the character uses should reflect his or her personality and approach to life as well as the social situation in which the speech takes place.

Dialogue can also reveal relationships. How two (or more) people speak to each other shows a lot about their feelings for each other. Do they give each other a turn to speak? What tones of voice do they use? Do they ask questions when they don't understand? Do they use polite phrases, slang that they both know, more than one language?

In terms of text organization, dialogue can help to break up narrative passages, and can be more interesting than reported speech.

Punctuating dialogue shows which words are the exact words that the speaker said. Follow these rules:

- Put quotation marks around the words each speaker says.
- If the tag line that identifies the speaker comes before the quotation, put a comma after it, before the quotation marks.
- If the tag line follows the quotation, put a comma inside the final quotation mark if the quotation ends with a period. If the quotation ends with a question mark or exclamation mark, skip the comma.
- If you place the tag line in the middle of the quotation, place a comma before it inside the quotation marks and after it, before the quotation marks.
- Start a new paragraph each time there is a new speaker, or if a speaker switches topics.

1. How does Piggy's speech differ from that of the other boys? What other distinctive speech characteristics do you note in the story?

2. Write a dialogue that you imagine might occur if you and some people you know were stranded together on a desert island. Pay attention both to each person's speech characteristics and to the dynamics between and among the participants.

Chapter 5

Beast from Water

Journal and Discussion Topics

1. What realization does Ralph have before the meeting?
2. What does Ralph remember that makes him flinch? Why does he react like that?
3. Do you think talking about fear will help or make things worse?
4. What does Piggy mean when he says, "There isn't no fear . . . unless we get frightened of people" (page 32)?
5. What do you think Simon is doing at night?
6. What is Simon trying to say at the meeting? How did you conclude this?
7. How does the boys' language change when Simon speaks?
8. Piggy asks if they're humans or animals or savages. How do you think he would define the differences?
9. What points does Jack make as he challenges Ralph's authority? Which, in your opinion, are valid? Which are not? Explain your thinking.
10. Do you think there is a beast? If so, what sort? What has led you to this conclusion?
11. What does Ralph's reference to three blind mice suggest to you?
12. Do you think Piggy's insights into Jack's character are valid? Explain.
13. Do you agree that adults stuck in the same situation as the boys would do better? Explain your thinking.

Summary

As Ralph tries to prepare for the meeting, he finds in himself an unaccustomed ennui, and is trapped in thoughts that, at first, he has no words to express. Suddenly, he sees himself with the eyes of his old self—and is aware of how far they have fallen away from the standards of personal care that they knew at home. With this new perspective, he is aware of the irregularity of the shape of the meeting place, the rocking log that none of them has thought to wedge. And this is followed by a clear realization of Piggy's value—his intellectual ability to reason logically. The others all come and sit down in the accustomed space, but Piggy stands outside the area to show his disapproval.

Ralph announces his purpose: to set things straight. He points out how decisions at the assembly don't get carried out in practice, for example, the decision to bring water. He then focuses on the three shelters. He reminds them that, although many helped with the first shelter, the third and last was built only by Ralph and Simon and is therefore not very strong and may not withstand violent weather. Next, he focuses on the lavatory area, which is no longer being used and reminds them that it's important not to use the area where the fruit grows for a toilet area. Finally he brings up the fire, and despite the hunters' laughter, insists that smoke is more important than pig, claiming melodramatically that without smoke they will die. So to assure the tending of the fire, he makes a new rule that the fire on the mountain will be the only fire on the island. The last topic that Ralph wants to discuss is the fear, which he dismisses, although he admits to feeling scared sometimes himself. He says that they can all talk about it, and when they've decided they can start over and take care of the fire and be happy again.

Jack takes the conch and immediately attacks the littluns, blaming them for starting the fear talk, calling them names, and reminding them that there "aren't any beasts to be afraid of on this island," although he is quick to add

both that it would serve the littluns right if they were caught by a beast and that he is a hunter and would have found the beast if it existed. He also makes the point that they're all afraid, but fear can't hurt you—it's just something you put up with.

Then Piggy takes the conch, saying that he agrees with some of what Jack says, and arguing against the existence of a beast. He says life is scientific, and there's nothing to be afraid of in the forest. He promises that if something goes wrong, there are people to put it right, unless, he says haltingly, they get "frightened of people." He then proposes to hear from a littlun who claims there is a beast and refute the claim with evidence.

Phil claims that he slept outside the shelter the previous night and saw something frightening in the trees. Ralph suggests that Phil had been dreaming, which Phil admits. Nevertheless, Phil claims that he knows which part of the awful stuff was nightmare and which part happened when he was awake. Ralph tells Phil he was asleep and there was no one there. But when Ralph asks the assembly, Simon volunteers that he had been out. When asked why, he begins to explain that he was going to a special place, when Jack calls out that Simon needed to get to the toilet area, and everyone laughs at Simon. Then Piggy calls forth another littlun, Percival, whose appearance reminds Ralph of the boy with the birthmark (whom no one has seen since the fire), although Ralph tries never to think of that boy. But while Piggy was able to coax that other boy into speech, Percival can only state his name and address, and then bursts into tears so deeply rooted that commands to stop do not reach him, and so intense that the other littluns begin to cry as well.

Maurice begins to clown, and gradually the littluns calm down. With repeated questions from Jack and Piggy, Percival finally says something inaudible that Jack repeats to the assembly: that "the beast comes out of the sea." Maurice speaks next, agreeing with Piggy that life is scientific and with Jack that fear is part of the human condition. But he's not convinced that Jack knows all about the wildlife on the island, and he's heard from his father that there are sea creatures that haven't yet been discovered. An argument ensues, and Ralph, who had hoped for consensus on the importance of the fire and a general agreement that there was no beast, feels that everything is coming apart. He takes back the conch from Maurice, and Simon takes it from him.

Simon, although terrified of speaking to a group, feels compelled to say the truth he believes: that perhaps there is a beast, and it is the boys themselves. Piggy is so shocked that he swears for the first time in the book. Simon is unable to articulate what he means, and in trying to convey his idea asks the others, "What's the dirtiest thing there is?" to which Jack answers in a one syllable word (presumably *shit* or a synonym) that makes the others laugh so hard that Simon is unable to go on.

But when there is silence again, someone suggests—out of turn—that maybe Simon means the beast is a kind of ghost. Ralph notices how dark it has become and how the littluns are huddling together. Piggy immediately takes the conch to refute the existence of ghosts. Ralph tries to stop the discussion of ghosts, realizing and saying that the discussion should have been carried on in the daytime. Someone else proposes—out of turn—that the beast is a ghost, and Ralph says they have to stop talking out of turn and breaking the rules. Then he apologizes for calling the assembly so late and, hoping to clear things up, invites a vote on ghosts, saying that he doesn't believe in them, or at least he doesn't think he does. But the vote shatters his hopes of resolution and finding out what's what.

Piggy snatches the conch to proclaim to all that he didn't vote for ghosts and trying to berate them back to sensibility, asking, "What are we? Humans? Or animals? Or savages?" Jack interrupts him with a personal attack, and when Ralph points out that Piggy has the conch, Jack attacks Ralph, Ralph's leadership, and the rules, finally making it clear that hunting is his chief priority and dashing away, followed by a large part of the group. Down to the beach they run, enacting a mock hunt, but the sounds that float back to the assembly place include not only laughter, but sounds of terror.

Piggy tries to convince Ralph to blow the conch, because otherwise they'll become animals soon. Ralph points out that if he blows and the others don't return, then the regime of order is clearly overturned immediately. Ralph suggests that he give up being chief, but Piggy argues that if Ralph steps down, Jack would feel free to carry his hatred of Piggy into action. Simon agrees that Ralph should stay chief, but Ralph isn't interested in Simon's opinion since Simon wouldn't say there wasn't a beast. Piggy tells Ralph that Jack hates Ralph as well, which surprises Ralph. Piggy explains that it arises from Jack's embarrassment over the fire and Jack's jealousy, and again Simon seconds Piggy.

As the talk ends, the three make a paean to adults, who know things and aren't afraid of the dark and are practical. Ralph cries out in a half prayer that he wishes a message would be sent them from the world of grownups. And as he wishes, they hear the cries of Percival, babbling his terror in the dark.

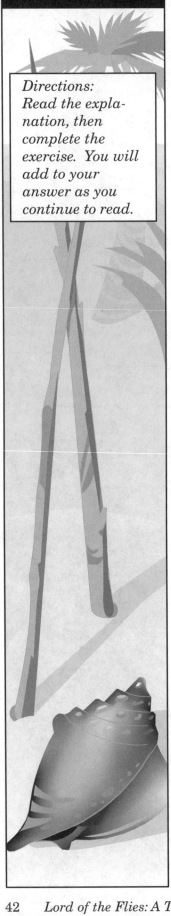

STRATEGY 10   Setting and Mood

Directions:
Read the expla-
nation, then
complete the
exercise. You will
add to your
answer as you
continue to read.

Setting refers to both the world in which the story takes place and the changing scenery that serves as the backdrop for each scene or chapter. Setting includes what the characters see, hear, smell, and can touch in their environment. Sights include:

- time of day
- season of the year
- plants and animals
- natural features

- weather
- landscape
- buildings or other structures

The general setting of this story is a deserted South Sea coral island with birds, pigs, and the diverse vegetation of a jungle.

Settings can serve different functions in different stories, and at different times in the same story. Setting may be a mere backdrop to the story, or it may have a more integral part. The setting may be symbolic and be a source of information about the inhabitants of the area. The setting may create conflicts for the characters of the story. The setting may help or hinder the characters in achieving their goal. It may provide materials or resources that help the characters solve problems, or create physical hardships or challenges that are difficult to overcome.

The setting of a story affects how we and the characters feel about their surroundings. This feeling is called **mood**. The setting can make things seem pleasant, or create an air of foreboding that hints to readers that something bad is about to happen.

Although a novel, like *Lord of the Flies,* is classified as a narrative—that is, a type of writing that tells a story—the sections of a novel that deal with the setting are usually passages of description. You may be aware of the shift back and forth from narrative to description as you read.

As you notice the setting, try to figure out what the writer is trying to convey. Pay attention to the possibilities and problems created by the setting, and the mood the setting creates for you in order to take advantage of hints the writer is giving about what might happen next.

Extend the following chart to create a record of *Lord of the Flies* settings and their function(s). Begin with Chapter 1.

Page #	Setting Description	Function(s) in Story

Writer's Forum 5   Persuasive Speech

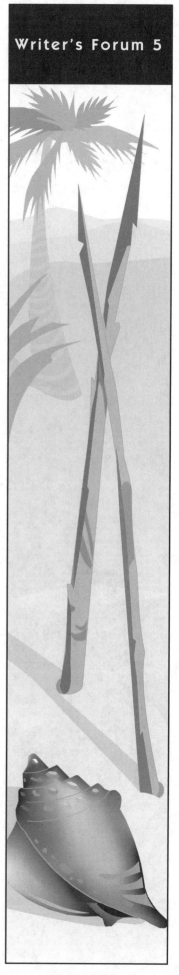

Persuasive discourse attempts to change what the audience thinks, believes, or values, or to move the audience to take action. In most persuasive discourse, the writer or speaker states a position and then provides evidence or reasons that attempt to convince the audience to embrace that position. Look back at the speech Ralph makes to the assembly about a third of the way into Chapter 2—page 37 in the Berkley edition— beginning with "Now we come to the most important thing" and ending with the boys rushing off to make a fire. This is an example of persuasion.

Writers and speakers use a variety of techniques to make their communications persuasive. Some of these techniques are logical and reasonable and accepted in our culture as examples of convincing argument. Other techniques that appeal to the audience's prejudices or to instincts that most people would consider base (like greed), may be used, but are often seen as inappropriate. Appeals to the audience's emotions are considered acceptable in some cases but not in others, and must be used carefully. Here are some examples of valid techniques for persuasion:

- Follow the standards for discourse in your community—make sure that your approach is courteous and presented in an appropriate forum. On the island, only the holder of the conch is supposed to have the floor.
- Tell the truth. If you cannot find convincing evidence, consider changing your point of view. Does Ralph stick to things he knows are true?
- Appeal to authority is a way to substantiate your claims. Make sure that the authority you cite is well respected. Usually when we talk about appealing to authority we mean a well-respected person or authoritative book. The authority of experience also carries a great deal of weight. What authority carries weight with those listening to Ralph?
- Use specific details, such as statistics and other numerical data. If you use numbers or other facts, verify them carefully. You have a responsibility to present accurate information. Are Ralph's claims likely? Does he provide any data to substantiate them?
- Make your point in several different ways. This will help ensure that you have communicated clearly and may help reinforce your point. Does Ralph need to reiterate his point?

Organization can be important in persuasion. Think carefully about the order in which you will present your evidence or arguments. Writers are often urged to put the most important reason first (or last), and then organize the other reasons in descending (or ascending) order of importance.

Knowing your audience is particularly important in persuasion. Knowing how their views differ from yours will show you what points you need to address. If you can anticipate their counter-arguments, you can forestall them by showing why they either don't apply or are not valid for some other reason.

1. In a persuasive essay written from the point of view of one of the boys, attempt to convince Ralph that he should remain chief. Use techniques from among those listed above.

Chapter 6

Beast from Air

Journal and Discussion Topics

1. How is the appearance of a "sign from the world of grown-ups" (page 106) ironic? What is the message the sign gives them?
2. Why didn't Ralph blow the conch (page 111)?
3. What kind of society and government is Jack endorsing in his challenge to Ralph?
4. What does Simon's "vision" tell him about "the beast"?
5. What do you think about Jack's response to the rocks?
6. What do you think happened to Ralph's mind when his idea was obscured?
7. What do you think will happen in Chapter 7? What leads you to think as you do?

Summary

The three boys—Ralph, Piggy, and Simon—find Percival, quiet him, and move him nearer the shelters. Then they go to sleep. During the night, Ralph's wish is answered: a battle is fought a short distance away from the island, and a sign from the world of adults—a dead pilot, still hanging from his parachute—is blown onto the mountain top. As the wind rises and falls, the figure is lifted up to a sitting position, and bowed down with its face to its knees again. . . . When the twins, who are on fire crew, wake up and find the fire out, they relight it and are relieved that their failure has escaped notice. Eric looks around and remembers the first fire, a thought he'd rather avoid. As he continues looking around while warming himself, he spies the dead man without being able to clearly identify what he sees. He alerts Sam, and after a few moments of raw terror, they flee down the mountain, hastening to wake up Ralph and tell him that they have seen the beast. The twins lie down in the shelter with Ralph and Piggy and Simon and wait till daylight in a world that, dark or light, now seems full of dangers.

At dawn, Ralph sends the twins to call an assembly, and when the boys are assembled, carrying their hunting spears, Ralph holds up the conch, but does not blow it, and hands it to the twins. They report a beast that sits up, that has claws, and that followed them and nearly touched one of them as it chased them down the mountain. Jack proposes a hunt, but Ralph thinks their wooden spears will be useless. Jack accuses him of fear, which Ralph readily admits. Ralph is concerned with making provision for the littluns while the hunters go to search for the beast but Jack says, "Sucks to the littluns!" Ralph decides to put Piggy in charge of them, which Jack interprets as favoritism, although Ralph points out that, being able to see with only one eye, Piggy can hardly hunt. Ralph then adds that this hunt will have to be undertaken differently than the hunts for pigs because the beast doesn't leave tracks, or they would have spotted it in the past.

Piggy asks what he and the littluns are to do if the beast comes upon them while the hunters are gone. Jack interrupts, and when Piggy retorts that he has the conch, Jack proclaims that the conch is no longer necessary because it's clear to everyone who ought to be allowed to speak and who—like Piggy, Simon, Bill, and Walter—should just stay quiet. Ralph feels that he must confront this, and orders Jack to sit down, but Jack, white-faced, remains standing, saying that finding the beast is a hunter's job. Ralph retorts that it requires more than hunters since the beast cannot be tracked, and that they must keep in mind the need to relight the fire, which must be out, unless they don't want to be rescued. This argument wins over the group to Ralph's camp once again. Ralph then consults Jack about where the beast might be and decides that they will go to the part of the island with the rocky bridge first—the one place Jack hasn't explored—then up the mountain to light the fire.

Ralph lets Jack lead the way to the "castle." Ralph orders the others to hide and goes across the bridge, but as he's crossing, Jack joins him. Ralph thinks the "castle" is a rotten place, but Jack immediately sees possibilities for a fort, focusing on the protection that could come from heaving the broken rocks down onto the heads of enemies. They find no beast, and return to the others who rush to explore the castle and work together to heave down a large rock, the beast forgotten. Ralph calls them back to their mission, but the impetus is lost. Jack leads and the rest come rebelliously.

STRATEGY 11

*Directions:
Read the expla-
nation, then
answer the ques-
tions.*

Symbolism is a technique in which a person, place, thing, or idea represents not only itself, but also a deeper more complex reality beyond itself. There are **universal** symbols that are true in many cultures and countries. A country's flag is a symbol of the country anywhere you go. The snake or serpent is a symbol of evil. Then there are **cultural/national** symbols that are understood within a particular society. Do any of you not know what a golden arch means? Universal and cultural/national symbolism involves allusion. You must know something else outside the story to interpret the symbol. Many universal symbols come from the Bible and Greek and Roman mythology, while many cultural/national symbols come from a particular nation's history and culture.

Finally, there are **contextual** symbols whose meaning applies only in the context of a particular work or works. For example, a conch is neither a universal symbol, nor is it—in our country at least—a cultural or national symbol. In *Lord of the Flies*, however, because the conch is literally the means of calling the group to assembly, it can be seen as a symbol of leadership, of the order and rules that come from home and the adult world, and of community commitment.

Symbolism can also operate on a larger level. **Allegory** is sustained symbolism carried throughout a work. Usually the characters in an allegory have symbolic meaning and may represent particular virtues or psychological states. The plot of the story is worked out in the usual way, but the story carries a second message about life that can be worked out by figuring out the symbolism.

It is necessary to be careful in deciding whether a work is allegorical or not. Sometimes it is useful to find out what the author thinks. Not that the author has the last say on all interpretation of a work. And although it is hard to make a case for allegory that is not intentional, people have worked through analyses of *The Lord of the Rings* as allegory despite the fact that J. R. R. Tolkien, the author, insisted that it was not. We have already established that *Lord of the Flies* uses symbolism. But is it an allegory? Golding himself said in a publicity questionnaire, "The whole book is symbolic in nature except . . . the end." This statement certainly gives us license to read the book as an allegory.

1. Try to work out an allegorical interpretation of *Lord of the Flies*. What might the four main characters—Ralph, Jack, Piggy, and Simon—stand for? What does the boys' experience on the island mean? How does the ending fit?

Test 2: Chapters 4–6

Vocabulary
Look at the group of words. Tell why it is important in the story.

1. sod you, nuts, bollocks _____

_____

Essay Topics

1. Who is/are the protagonist(s) in this book? What do you think are the most important conflicts in this plot? Explain your thinking.

2. How do you define *community?* In light of your definition, give a critique of the boys' success in creating community.

3. Do you like Ralph? Piggy? Explain why you do or don't like each boy.

4. If you were writing this story, what would happen next? Explain how you would develop the plot.

5. Imagine the boys' lives before they left England. What do you suppose the boys are lacking from their "normal" life at home? If you were in their situation, what would you miss most?

6. What are the weaknesses in Ralph's government?

Chapter 7   Shadows and Tall Trees

Journal and Discussion Topics

1. What is the import to you of Ralph's revelry about washing?
2. Why did Simon interrupt Ralph's meditation on the ocean? What do you think made Simon speak? Do you think Ralph *will* get back? Does Ralph?
3. Why do you think that Golding used the analogy, "Jack bent down to them as though he loved them" of pig droppings?
4. What are some reasons people imagine or fantasize about something not present? Why do you think Ralph indulges in memories so often?
5. In your own words, summarize the interpersonal interactions that take place in between Jack's statement "He's gone" (page 128) and "use a littlun" on page 130. What do you think of this "game"?
6. Why do you think the narrator adds, "The only trouble was that he would never be a very good chess player" (page 132) after comparing Ralph to a chess strategist? Why wouldn't Ralph be a good one?
7. Why does Jack say, "We mustn't let anything happen to Piggy, must we?"
8. Why is the narrator's comment, "as though something indecent had been said," (page 134) ironic?
9. Were you surprised that Roger chose to accompany Jack and Ralph up the mountain? Explain your reaction.
10. Compare and contrast the approaches of Jack, Ralph, and Roger to dealing with checking the top of the mountain for the beast and their responses to what they found atop the mountain. What is your reaction to their attitudes? How does the point of view contribute to your reaction?

Summary

Sitting down to eat, Ralph daydreams a complete clean-up: washing his clothes, cutting his hair, bathing, etc. He looks over the other boys, and applies the standards of homelife to them, realizing that he takes the current situation as normal now and, moreover, doesn't care. He is looking out to sea, overwhelmed by the vastness of the ocean, when Simon softly tells him that he'll get back home.

Roger interrupts them, and they go to meet Jack. Jack has found droppings, which he "bent down to . . . as though he loved them." Since the chase is going the same direction they are, Ralph agrees that they can hunt on the way to the mountain. Ralph uses the time to daydream, recalling in minute detail comforting details from his past life at home, when suddenly a boar rushes into their midst. Ralph's spear hits the boar's snout, Jack is wounded, and another argument erupts between them, quelled by Robert, who suddenly pretends to be the boar hit by Ralph's spear. A mock hunt evolves, the hunters beating Robert, but soon his cries have become real cries of pain. The hunters grab him, Ralph joins in the jabbing, and someone yells, "Kill him!" and the ritual chant begins, while Jack holds Robert's hair and wields his knife. Even Ralph wants to join in the attack, but Jack lowers his arm and the ritual is over. Jack says it was a good game, but Ralph is uneasy. They discuss how they can improve the game, and Robert says they want a real pig so they can kill it, but Jack says, "Use a littlun," at which everyone laughs.

Ralph calls their attention back to their mission, but the others suggest returning to Piggy before dark. Jack points out that Ralph can't start the fire anyway, since they don't have Piggy's specs. They don't come out in the spot they are aiming for, and they realize that they won't get back till after dark. Ralph says someone must go back with a message, and Simon volunteers. Ralph consults Jack about using a pig-run, and for the first time, recognizes that Jack's antagonism comes out every time that he's not leading. In this conversation, the antagonism grows to the point that Ralph confronts it, saying to Jack, "Why do you hate me?" But there is no response, so they go on.

When they reach the mountain, Ralph points out that there won't be light by the time they climb up, but Jack challenges his courage and starts up himself, so Ralph joins him, and Roger, too, comes along. Ralph says they're foolish to go up only three of them, and Jack says he'll go himself, implying that Ralph is too frightened. Jack goes, and comes back shaking, barely able to speak. He describes a thing that "bulges," but Ralph says no creature bulges, and all three go up to look. They creep up on all fours, and when Jack points out the thing, Ralph stands up to see the apelike thing with a ruined face lift its head to face him. All three drop their spears and race down the mountain.

STRATEGY 12

Foreshadowing and Flashback

*Directions:
Read the expla-
nation. Then
answer the ques-
tions. For the
second question,
you will have to
read beyond this
chapter before
you can answer.*

Writers do not always tell plot events in chronological order. For one thing, they may hint at events before they occur. This is called **foreshadowing**, and it lets readers know beforehand something about what is going to happen later. This technique helps create suspense and irony and keeps the reader involved in the unfolding plot.

Foreshadowing may come from a character, from the setting, or from the narrator. Simon's statement to Ralph that he'll get home may be foreshadowing or may not—it's not possible to tell yet from the plot development at this point. But we might go back to the two elements of the setting mentioned in Strategy 3—the "witchlike cry" and the "skull-like coconuts" and now say (perhaps) that they foreshadowed something. The narrator's foreshadowing is very subtle in this book. For example, two pages after Jack says in Chapter 2 "After all, we're not savages. We're English . . . So we've got to do the right things." (page 44), the narrator uses the word *savage* twice—to describe the forest filled with flame, and to describe Ralph. The narrator, by using the word that Jack decried, foreshadows the changes in behavior to come.

Writers may also go back to material that happened prior to the beginning of the story or earlier in the plot sequence. This is called **flashback**. Flashbacks give the reader necessary background material to understand the story or reiterates important material. Flashbacks may come from the narrator or the characters. When Ralph (page 95) recalls the little boy with the mulberry-colored birthmark and pushes the memory away, Ralph has had a flashback. All of the background information that we get (and most of it is about Piggy's and Ralph's family history) comes through dialogue. Flashback from the narrator is notably missing from this work, except in Ralph's reveries, as though the boys are completely cut off from life before the landing on the island.

1. Find another example of a character having a flashback. What information does it contain?

2. As you continue reading find as many examples as you can of foreshadowing. Are they from characters, the setting, or the narrator? Did you realize they were foreshadowings when you read them, or only later?

Chapter 8

Gift for the Darkness

Journal and Discussion Topics

1. What does Ralph's blasphemous answer to Piggy's question, "D'you think we're safe down here?" indicate to you?
2. What factors contribute to Jack's departure from "Ralph's lot"?
3. Who is the first to realize that Jack might prove dangerous?
4. What are the implications of Jack's using the word *play* in "I'm not going to play any longer"?
5. Jack's choir are all (except Simon) back with him, having accepted him as leader, by the end of the chapter. Why doesn't Jack get support at the meeting? Why does the narrator refer to their voices as they had used to sound in the choir (page 151)?
6. How does Ralph react to the new situation? Piggy?
7. The first gift in the book is noted here. What does it signify?
8. Piggy has insight into many things. What do you think of his comments about Simon?
9. Summarize Simon's experiences in your own words. Why did he go under the mat in the first place? What insight did he have?
10. Compare and contrast Simon's, Jack's, Piggy's, and Ralph's reactions to the beast's presence on the mountain.
11. Analyze the description of the death of the pig.
12. What does the sow's head represent to Jack? To Simon? To you?
13. In Chapter 2, Ralph said, "This is a good island." By Chapter 8, he believes that "the island was getting worse and worse" (page 158). Is the island changing? What is he trying to convey?
14. What is Ralph afraid of?
15. What effect did the paint and costume have on Jack?
16. Why did Piggy run away when Jack and his hunters came to steal the fire?
17. Compare and contrast Ralph's regime with Jack's.
18. Explain what the Lord of the Flies said to Simon.

Summary

The boys are back by the shelters, miserable and not knowing what to do. Ralph interprets the "thing's" choice of seat as showing that it doesn't want them to have a fire, and hence doesn't want them to be rescued. Jack interrupts twice to ask about his hunters, and Ralph—so frightened and at his wits end that he's already sworn at Piggy—dismisses the hunters as "boys with sticks." Jack turns red and walks away. Piggy immediately senses that this is a breaking point, and even as he is conveying this to Ralph, Jack blows the conch. Ralph goes to the meeting place and tries to begin the meeting himself, but Jack won't let him. Jack begins by telling the group that they saw the beast, and then goes on to say that Ralph has said the hunters are no good. Ralph protests, but Jack goes on. He accuses Ralph of being like Piggy, and not a proper chief, telling the hunters that Ralph did not go up to the top when he and Roger did. Ralph protests, but Jack goes on, saying that Ralph isn't a proper hunter because he hasn't ever gotten meat for the group. He calls for a vote against Ralph. But he doesn't get support. Saying, "I'm not going to play any longer. Not with you…. Anyone who wants to hunt when I do can come too," he walks away crying tears of anger and humiliation. Ralph calls out, "Jack!" but this doesn't stop him.

After a pause, Ralph realizes that Piggy is speaking to him, urging that they decide what can be done. To everyone's surprise, Simon takes the conch and suggests that they go up the mountain, but the suggestion meets with derision. Piggy takes up the conch and goes on with his plan. He suggests a fire near the bathing pool and shelters. Ralph accepts this idea, although he points out that the smoke won't show as much. They go to make the fire, and even Piggy helps fetch wood, lighting the fire himself with his one remaining lens. The littluns dance around the fire and Ralph, after finishing the work talks briefly with Piggy about keeping up the fire. But when he gets to the point of mentioning fire duty, Piggy points out that just about all the bigger boys are gone. Piggy thinks they can make out with just the two of them and the twins, but Ralph sits and worries. Piggy and the twins go into the woods and gather fruit and bring it to Ralph and they all eat. Then suddenly Ralph realizes that Simon's gone and asks if the others think that he's climbing the mountain. Piggy retorts that Simon might be because he's crazy. Actually, Simon is again in his leafy hiding place.

Meanwhile on the beach, Jack is standing before the former choir (except for Simon), and the boys who once sang like angels have become hunters. Jack announces himself as chief and is accepted. He then states as edicts two things over which he has no control—that they will forget about the beast and that they won't dream (by which he means, "have nightmares") as much in this new location—and the others passionately agree. He then states his plan of action: to lure more of the biguns away from "the conch and all that," and without anyone noticing that he has done so. He flatly contradicts his statement that they will forget the beast by saying that whenever they go hunting they'll leave some of the meat for it in propitiation because maybe then it will leave them alone. They leave on a hunt, with Jack leading, and find a whole group of pigs, resting unsuspiciously. Of the whole group, Jack unaccountably chooses a nursing mother to kill. On his count they throw their spears, two of which lodge in her flank, and then chase her, catch her, and stab at her with incredible cruelty, Roger pushing a spear up her anus until Jack cuts her throat and ends her life.

And shortly the boys are laughing uncontrollably at Maurice (playing the pig) and Robert (playing Roger) reenacting the spear thrust. After Jack guts the pig, Roger asks how they can make a fire, and Jack proposes a raid. He then tells Roger to sharpen a stick at both ends, has him jam one end in a crack in a rock, and impales the pig's head on the end as an offering for the beast.

It turns out that Simon's hideout is so nearby that when his eyes are open, he is looking directly at the pig's head. And a conversation begins between them. The head tells him to return to the others, but Simon stays where he is, and the flies that have been drinking the pig's blood come to rest on him, after which the narrator identifies the pig's head as the Lord of the Flies.

Meanwhile Ralph and Piggy see that it's going to rain and try to figure out how to keep the fire going. Piggy points out that with Samneric sharing a turn rather than taking two turns, there aren't enough people. Ralph considers again the lack in himself of the ability to think like a grown-up, and continuing to identify the human situation with the quality of the island, thinks to himself, "the island was getting worse and worse." He tells Piggy that sometimes he himself doesn't care, and he's afraid of becoming like the others. Piggy has no answer except to go on. That, he believes, is what grown-ups would do. Ralph asks Piggy what he thinks is the cause of things gone wrong, and Piggy responds that he thinks Jack is at the root of the trouble. Immediately, Jack, Maurice, and Robert and "two anonymous savages" come racing out of the forest, referred to by the narrator as "demoniac figures" and several times as "savages," and Ralph notices that Piggy runs away. The two unidentified savages seize flaming branches from the fire and flee. The other three stop, and Jack, naked except for paint and a belt, issues an invitation to join his tribe, although he doesn't guarantee admittance. Jack invites them to come join in feasting on the pig, and after being cued several times, Robert and Maurice announce together, "The Chief has spoken," and they leave.

Piggy, who has returned bringing the conch, explains to Ralph that he was sure that was what Jack was after, and they move to the assembly area. Ralph begins to speak and explain that Jack's group raided them for fire, but he loses his train of thought several times, and looks to Piggy for help. Several of the biguns propose going to the feast, and when Ralph proposes that they get their own meat, they explain that they don't want to go into the jungle—the others are hunters, one of the remaining biguns says, and that makes it different for them.

Meanwhile, Simon is listening to the Lord of the Flies, who tells Simon that the others think he's batty. The Lord of the Flies claims to be the beast, to which Simon replies (with difficulty because he is suffering from heat and the onset of an epileptic seizure) that the "beast" is only a "pig's head on a stick." The head responds with amusement to the idea that the beast can be killed. He tells Simon, "I'm part of you. . . . I'm the reason why it's no go. . . ." He continues by saying that there is no escape, and that there will be fun or else Jack, Roger, Maurice, Robert, Bill, Piggy, and Ralph will all "do" him (kill him). But by this time, Simon's seizure has taken over his body, and he falls down and loses consciousness.

Chapter 9

A View to a Death

Journal and Discussion Topics

1. How would you characterize Jack's regime? What details support your conclusions?
2. Why does the narrator refer to Simon as "the beast"? What effect does this have for you?
3. Simon's death could be considered symbolic. Looked at this way, what might the death of Simon symbolize?
4. In what ways is Simon's death ironic?
5. How do you think the boys will react to their role in Simon's death?

Summary

The clouds build up over the island, and in the oppressive atmosphere, the narrator tells us, "nothing prospered but the flies who blackened their lord." Simon passes from the seizure state into sleep and upon waking, he arises. Looking at the Lord of the Flies, he repeats his question to the assembly: "What else is there to do?" And although weak and weary, he begins to climb up the mountain. Reaching the top, he spies the humped thing looking at him. Hiding his face, he continues upwards. Here, too, the flies have alit in droves. Simon can see the rotting flesh on the body that is held together only because of the parachute and clothing, and he is sick to his stomach. Then he frees the parachute lines so that the figure is freed. Then he spots the boys and starts staggering down the mountain to tell them that the beast is "harmless and horrible."

Meanwhile Ralph and Piggy are bathing, waiting for the rain to come and relieve the oppression in the air. Ralph suddenly realizes that people are missing. He asks aloud where Samneric and Bill are, and Piggy points to Jack's party. Piggy says they've gone for the meat, and Ralph adds for hunting, being a tribe, and war-paint. Piggy suggests that they go too to make sure nothing happens. When they arrive, everyone else is already there eating pig, except Simon, and Jack is sitting on a log throne "like an idol."

Ralph and Piggy are uncomfortable, but when Piggy gets burnt by boys removing meat from the fire and he yells and dances in pain, he becomes "once more the center of social derision so that everyone felt cheerful and normal." Jack commands that Piggy and Ralph be given meat, orders himself a drink, and when the boys are done, orders everyone to sit down and asks who plans to join his tribe for the food and protection. Ralph responds that he was chosen and the goal was to keep the fire going and now all the boys are just going where the meat is. Jack pointedly notes the meat in Ralph's hand, and Ralph is mortified. Ralph finally claims the authority of the conch, and Jack counters that Ralph hasn't got the conch with him. Boys begin responding to Jack's membership offer, and Piggy warns Ralph that they should leave. At that moment lightning and thunder crash in the sky and Ralph taunts Jack with the tribe's lack of shelters. In this case, as in all times of doubt and fear, Jack calls for the dance. This time Roger plays the pig while Jack represents himself, and the storm is so frightening that Piggy and Ralph join in just to be close to the others, but this time the chant goes "Kill the beast! Cut his throat! Spill his blood!" Roger changes to a hunter role and the circle of dancers is empty. Then a beast stumbles out of the forest and into the center of the group, crying out about a body on a hill, while the boys hit it with sticks until it falls over a lip of rock to the sand by the water. The boys follow it down and tear it apart. When the rain starts, the boys break apart and notice how small the beast is. At the same time, the parachute on the mountain top fills with wind, and the figure slides down the mountain onto the beach, driving the boys screaming before it, and then goes out to sea. The other little beast lies on the beach, its blood staining the sand, until Simon is lifted by the water, and making a silver shape on the surface, drifts out to the sea.

Strategy 13   Names and Euphemisms

*Directions:
Read the expla-
nation. Then
answer the ques-
tion. You will
need to read
beyond this
chapter before
you can complete
your answer.*

Character names (and place names) can be symbolic or descriptive. We have already seen (Strategy 5) that the names of Ralph, Jack, and Simon have a special meaning because of their association with *The Coral Island*. Names can also have a meaning based on the literal meaning of the word in the original language from which the name comes or connected to a real person who had that name.

One way to see if symbolic meaning is being used in a story is to test a few names and see if the connections add meaning. Since we are expecting the characters to be symbolic (see Strategy 11), we might expect to find that their names characterize their role or what they symbolize. The nickname *Jack* is related to the name *Jacob,* meaning "supplanter," someone who replaces another by force or treachery. One meaning of the shortened name *Ralph*, which is connected with *Randolph,* is "disinterested help." *Simon* means "attentive."

1. Make a case for the fit of the meaning of each of the three names *(Jack, Ralph, Simon)* to the character.

2. *Roger* means "famous spear." When you have finished the book, write a paragraph telling why or why not the meaning of this name is helpful in understanding Roger and his role.

Anti-Euphemism

A **euphemism** is an inoffensive word substituted for a harsh or blunt one. A common euphemism is "passed away" as a substitute for "died." So, by extension, an **anti-euphemism** (a term I just made up) is a particular form of verbal abuse in which an offensive term is substituted for an inoffensive one. The chief example of this is *Piggy*. Although he manages, through Ralph's good will (if it can be called that), to avoid being called *Fatty* (except by Jack on page 77), we never learn the real name of this important character. Nobody cares enough to find out.

3. In one sense Piggy's name represents something about him—his girth. When you are done with the novel, examine whether there is any other meaning to the name Piggy, for example, a connection between this boy and the only kind of island fauna, besides gulls, that is ever identified by species. Write a brief report of your thoughts.

Namelessness

One of the most obvious things about names in this book is that so many of them are missing. So far, no adult has been named, Ralph's daddy and Piggy's auntie included. The little 'uns (*littluns* beginning in Chapter 3) are not named individually, but lumped unceremoniously together in a way that constantly recalls the irresponsibility that does not bother to name and count them. The boy with the mulberry-colored birthmark was not named. No plant or animal that lives on the island, with the exception of pigs and gulls, is named.

4. When you have finished the book, compare and contrast the meaning of the three main kinds of namelessness: the namelessness of adults; the namelessness of children; the namelessness of plants and animals on the island.

5. Sam and Eric are not nameless, but their names become a blur. What meaning do you attach to this?

Writer's Forum 6

Compare and Contrast Essay

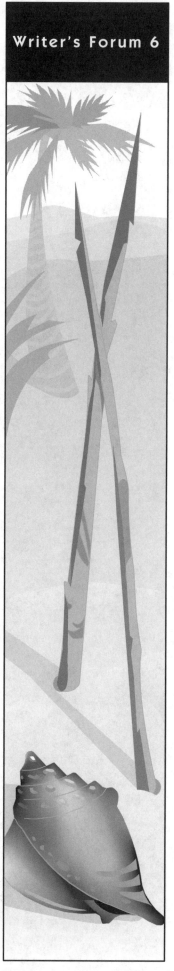

Comparing and **contrasting** puts two or more subjects side by side in order to draw insights from their similarities and differences.

In a compare and contrast essay, you show the similarities and differences between two people, things, ideas, approaches, etc., and draw some conclusion based on this examination. You choose the categories to compare and contrast based on your purpose, and these categories will change depending on your topic. For example, if you were comparing and contrasting Piggy and Ralph, you might choose categories such as "maturity," "wisdom," "charisma," and "appearance." If, however, you were contrasting Jack's government with Ralph's government, you would use different categories, perhaps: "goals," "rules," "effectiveness," "fairness," etc. A Venn diagram or a chart can help you organize the information you will use. A Venn diagram shows visually what two or more subjects have in common and what characteristics they have that they do not share.

Here is an example:

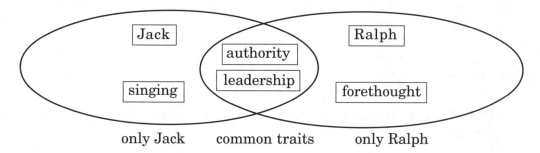

only Jack   common traits   only Ralph

Words that can help you express concepts of similarity and difference include the following:

SIMILARITY

- as well as
- similarly
- likewise
- alike
- at the same time
- resemble

DIFFERENCE

- differ
- whereas
- however
- while
- but
- on the contrary
- conversely
- though
- on the other hand

1. Make a list of the categories you would use to compare and contrast Piggy's idea of the adult society from which the boys came with the society they create on the island.

2. Write an essay comparing and contrasting Piggy and Ralph.

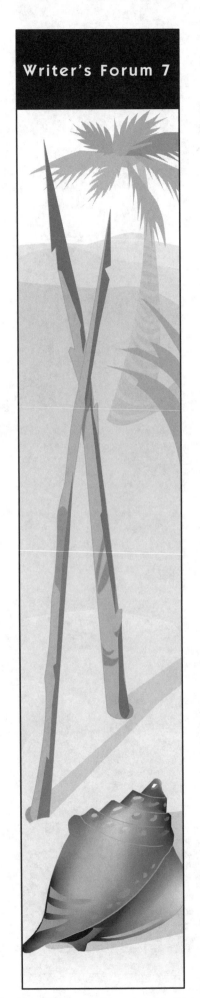

Writer's Forum 7

Poet W. H. Auden spoke of poetry as a "game of knowledge, a bringing to consciousness, by naming them, of emotions and their hidden relationships." Thinking of poetry as a game we play with the poet can help us understand a genre that no one can clearly define.

The poet gives us sounds and sense set in a shape on a sheet of paper. The sounds include rhythms and repetitions. Saying the poem aloud several times will help you find its sound. The sense includes literal and figurative language, imagery, made-up words, onomatopoeia, double meanings and constructions that break the rules we usually follow for using language. The shape on the page helps us know how to read the poem. We enter the game and see what happens; we play with the sense and sound to not only find, but also to FEEL, meaning.

One important element of the poem is the meter. The meter is composed of one or more units called "feet."

    one foot = monometer
    two feet = dimeter
    three feet = trimeter
    four feet = tetrameter
    five feet = pentameter
    six feet = hexameter

A "foot" is a combination of accented and unaccented syllables. The standard feet in English are as follows:

    anapest   duh duh DUM
    dactyl   DUM duh duh
    iamb   duh DUM
    trochee   DUM duh
    spondee   DUM DUM
    Double-iamb   duh duh DUM DUM (counts as two feet)

Another important element of a poem is the relationship between the sound and the sense, and this relationship is unique, depending on the subject of the poem and the speaker. The poet may be, but often is not, the speaker in the poem. The speaker is often an imaginary person, a "persona." The sound of the poem—the vowel and consonant combinations in the words, the accents, the rhythm and meter—are connected in each case to the meaning, and to the minds and hearts of the characters who are the speakers.

1. An elegy is a poem mourning someone's death. Write a poem about Simon's death. If you wish, make it from the point of view of one of the boys.

Test 3: Chapters 7–9

Vocabulary

Look at the group of words. Tell why it is important in the story.

1. windy, infuriating, impervious, bravado _____

   _____

Essay Topics

1. If you were Simon and there had been an opportunity to recount your encounter with the Lord of the Flies before you went down to the beach, what would you have told?

2. How does Golding use dialogue in creating characterizations?

3. What does the conch symbolize?

4. What factors led to Simon's death?

5. Did any of your opinions about the characters or ideas about how the plot would happen change after the mother pig was killed? Explain your thoughts.

6. How does Golding use "dark" or "darkness" and "light"?

Chapter 10   The Shell and the Glasses

Journal and Discussion Topics

1. Why do you think the narrator mentions "impaired sight" and "befouled bodies" (page 179)?
2. Analyze how Piggy, Ralph, and Samneric deal with Simon's death.
3. How does Jack's reaction to Simon's death differ from the reaction of his followers?
4. How is the word *savage* used differently in this chapter than before?
5. What meaning do you attach to the episode involving the beating of Wilfrid?
6. What hint about the war in the world they left is given in Chapter 10? What does it mean to you?
7. What do you think is happening to Ralph when the "curtain flaps" in his mind?
8. How did you react to Ralph's prayer (page 192)?
9. Describe as well as you can what happened during the fight.
10. When did you realize what Jack and his hunters came for?
11. Why does the narrator say "He was a chief now in truth" (page 194)?
12. What is the significance of face paint in this chapter? In the story?

Summary

Ralph, with a black eye and a cut knee, approaches Piggy in the morning and asks if he's the only one left. Piggy tells him that there are some littluns and Samneric. Ralph says a word, and since Piggy doesn't hear him, repeats it—it is *Simon*. Ralph asks Piggy what to do. Piggy nods to the conch, but Ralph laughs at the idea of calling an assembly. Ralph says again to Piggy, "That was Simon"; and then "that was murder." Piggy argues against Ralph's characterization, blaming the dance, the darkness, the weather, and the fear. Ralph can't identify what he felt, but he says he wasn't scared. Piggy insists it wasn't "what [Ralph] said," and suggests that Simon is still alive and was pretending, but Ralph is adamant. Then he says Piggy was outside the circle and suggests that perhaps Piggy didn't fully see what happened. Piggy latches onto this, saying he couldn't see, and then saying it was an accident and blaming Simon for crawling around in the dark. "He asked for it," Piggy concludes. But Ralph does not accept Piggy's explanation, crying out "I'm frightened. Of us. I want to go home. Oh God, I want to go home." Piggy tells Ralph that not everyone saw them at the feast and they should pretend they weren't at the dance. Anyway, Piggy concludes, Ralph himself had noticed that Piggy remained on the outside; and now, finally, Ralph gives in to the lies, muttering that he, too, was on the outside and Piggy eagerly reinforces the story. The two boys encounter Samneric, who flush and don't meet Ralph's eyes when he greets them. All four boys lie to each other, claiming to have left the feast early before the dance.

The scene shifts to Castle Rock, as Roger approaches. Roger is admitted and admires the arrangement by which a large rock can be dropped on the head of anyone who approaches. Robert mentions with a giggle that Wilfrid is tied up waiting for a beating, and he doesn't know why. Roger sits and ponders, intrigued with the "possibilities of irresponsible authority." Then he goes to join the tribe, who now are referred to as *savages* (and Jack as *chief*). The chief announces his plan to hunt the following day, taking a few hunters and leaving the rest to guard their gate from "the others," who may try to sneak in, and from the beast. Stanley inarticulately tries to ask the chief if they hadn't killed the beast for good the previous evening, but the chief exclaims, "No! How could we—kill—it!?" The conversation continues and the chief says they will feast after the hunt, and Bill raises the question of how they will light a fire. The chief announces that on this very night they will go with two hunters and take fire from the others.

Shifting back to the beach, we find the boys relighting a fire made of damp wood. They are still thinking about Simon. They agree that it would be better to be taken prisoner by the "Reds"—the enemy in the adult war—than by Jack's tribe. Ralph's trouble keeping order in his mind and remembering the importance of the fire is growing. Facing the opposition of the three others to keeping the fire going all the time, Ralph agrees that they can let it go out for the night because, as Piggy points out, they can always light it again in the morning. They go to bed, but their rest is disturbed, first by Sam and Eric who, roused by something, are mistakenly fighting each other. Sometime later, Piggy awakens Ralph when he hears noise outside. Ralph is so terrified that he prays "that the beast would prefer littluns." The thing outside calls for Piggy, whose fear brings on an asthma attack. Then the tent is attacked and a fight ensues. Matching up the description of the fight and the boys' descriptions of their injuries makes it seem likely that Ralph and Eric were fighting each other, rather than Jack and his hunters, whom they've identified as the assailants. Ralph checks on everyone, finally asking Piggy if he's okay. Piggy says he thought they wanted the conch, but Ralph finds it still in its place when he checks. It is only then that they find out what the hunters have taken: Piggy's broken glasses, which make Jack "a chief now in truth."

Chapter 11

Castle Rock

Journal and Discussion Topics

1. Ralph asks "are we savages or what?" What do you think he means by the question?
2. In Ralph's speech, he says, "Then there was, there was.... that's his fault too." What does he have in mind? Do you agree with his analysis?
3. Do you believe Ralph and Piggy and Samneric would have given the others fire if they'd asked? Explain your thinking.
4. How do you interpret Ralph's statement, "we can't ever be rescued"?
5. Characterize the change that takes place in Piggy with the loss of his glasses.
6. What is the "one thing [that Jack] hasn't got" that Piggy plans to show him?
7. What do you think is the connection between paint and savagery?
8. Do you think it's true that they can't be rescued without smoke?
9. Why do Piggy and Ralph lie to each other (page 200)? What's the impact on Samneric?
10. What foreshadows Piggy's death?
11. Why is Ralph's reference to "playing the game" ironic?
12. Why does the narrator say "Samneric protested out of the heart of civilization"?
13. What struck you most about the description of Piggy's death?
14. What has changed in the way Roger acts? Why didn't he show this side of himself before?
15. What does it mean that Jack hurled his spear at Ralph "with full intention"?

Summary

On the beach, the four boys try to bring their dead fire back to life. With Piggy effectively blinded and no fire, they need to rethink things. At Piggy's suggestion, Ralph blows the conch, and the four of them hold an assembly. After an introduction by Piggy, Ralph begins to speak. He emphasizes how simple their plan was: to keep a fire going so that the smoke would help them be rescued. He alludes to Simon's death, blaming Jack, and claims that he would have shared fire with the hunters if they'd asked. Now, he says, "we can't ever be rescued." Ralph gets lost in the haze of his mind, and Piggy recalls him to reality. They plan to face-off with the tribe. Piggy is the only one who won't take a spear, since he'll have to be led anyway. And now Piggy says what he wouldn't listen to Ralph say earlier—that Simon was murdered—and he recalls the young boy with the birthmark on his face. The others warn him that he might get hurt, but he brushes them off, saying, "What can he do more than he has?" Piggy just asks to carry the conch. He says, "I'll show him the one thing he hasn't got." He plans to point out that he is weak, sickly, and blind, while Jack is none of these, but "what's right's right"—and demand his glasses back. Ralph agrees to support Piggy (remembering what Simon had said to him by the rocks), while Sam and Eric warn that it will be hard to face Jack with his warpaint on. They prepare by eating from the now "devastated" fruit trees, the suggestion being that soon they will not have enough food. Eric and Sam seem to want to put on paint, to be on an equal footing with the others, but Ralph refuses, and again focuses on the need for smoke. And for the first time, it is clear to the others besides Piggy that Ralph has forgotten why they need smoke. Ralph denies that he has forgotten, and Piggy tries to support him by lying, "You remember everything." But the twins are disturbed and worried.

They start off on their quest, Ralph first with his spear, the twins next, and Piggy behind, following the twins' trailing spear butts and carrying the conch. They spot the smoke and step into the open, and Ralph takes the conch and sounds it. Roger, guarding the lever, is on the cliff, and he leads the others in beginning to pelt the four visitors with small stones. Sam almost falls, and Roger begins to feel a great power. Ralph calls for Jack, just as he is coming up behind them from the forest. The four boys turn to Jack, and the twins dart behind Ralph for safety, and now stand nearest the entrance. Ralph tells Jack that he's "got to" return Piggy's specs and calls Jack a thief. Jack rushes at Ralph with his spear, but Ralph blocks the blow and hits Jack in the face. They face off again and Jack's spear hits Ralph's fingers. At Piggy's reminder of their objectives, Ralph grounds his spear butt and restates his goals: the return of Piggy's specs and enough people to keep the fire going. Jack orders his savages to grab Samneric, who protest, the narrator tells us, "out of the heart of civilization." They are taken and tied up. Jack, knowing that Ralph will try to rescue the twins, strikes out and catches Ralph unexpectedly on the ear. Ralph hits Jack in the stomach. In the pause that follows, Piggy demands a chance to speak and waves the conch. Roger, one hand on the lever, again begins his pelting.

Piggy begins by telling the savages that they are acting like kids. He contrasts Ralph's and Jack's governments, and Ralph joins in, but soon cannot make himself heard. Then Roger leans on the lever. The rock shatters the conch and knocks Piggy off the rock bridge He falls forty feet down to land on his back on a rock. His skull is cracked, his brains spill out, the water washes over him, and he is gone. Jack throws a spear at Ralph's chest, intending to kill him. The spear causes a superficial wound, but others are thrown after it, and Ralph turns and runs away. As he flees, he passes the sow's head on the stick, but the tribe stops there, and the chief orders them back to their headquarters. He pauses at the entrance to berate Samneric for approaching armed, and orders them to join the tribe. He begins poking them with a spear. Then Roger comes up and the implication is there that he will torture them until they agree to join.

STRATEGY 14

*Directions:
Read the expla-
nation, then
complete the
exercises. The
second exercise
will not be fin-
ished until you
have read the
entire book.*

We often speak of **character traits** as absolutes—that is, characters either have them or not. So we might describe a character as intelligent and outspoken. This is useful for a start. But even a character that we recognize as intelligent and outspoken in general can be more or less outspoken and act more or less rationally, depending on the situation. Considering the variations in character traits can be the first step in taking a more realistic view of the complex thing we call character. We can think about character traits as existing on a continuum, a scale with opposite traits at the ends and a whole range of possible points in between. For example:

honest————————————————————————————————deceptive

independent_____seeking favor

Think about Piggy: he is presented initially as a boy who is honest and frank, even to the point of being outspoken, criticizing the others for acting "like kids," although it clearly can't do him any good in their eyes. Now look back at the section of "The Shell and the Glasses" (pages 180–182), where it describes Piggy participating with Ralph and Samneric in a group lie that removes them from culpability in Simon's death. But when his glasses are stolen, Piggy seems to feel that he has nothing to lose, and his frankness returns. "Young Simon was murdered," he says. "And there was that other kid what had a mark on his face. Who's seen him since we first come here?" (page 197). You can see that Piggy's traits are responsive to circumstances, and that to say that Piggy is or isn't honest would not come near to telling the whole story.

1. For each continuum, write a paragraph telling how the character(s) indicated move(s) along it during the course of the book.

   self-concerned————————————————community-minded
   (Jack/Samneric)

   clear-thinking————————————————confused
   (Ralph)

   kind_____cruel
   (Jack/Ralph)

2. Choose a single character and write a full-page description of his character traits. Explain how his behavior varies along each continuum that you identify. Use the information you have acquired so far, and add to your description as you finish the book.

Writer's Forum 8   A Possible Ending

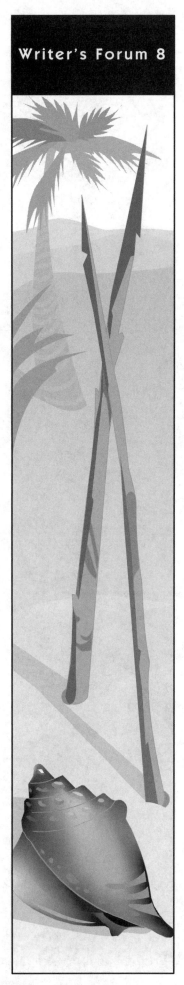

The end of a book is a special part because it usually is meant to round off all the little details and plot bits; explain what needs explanation; put a final exclamation point on the themes; leave the characters in a situation of equilibrium or show their disequilibrium in a striking way, noting what has happened to all the important characters; and send the reader off feeling that all loose ends have been tied up or that the situation is so complex and tangled that no neat ending is possible. The ending should make sense of the foreshadowings and plot development that have occurred so far in the book, and play out the main ideas that have been treated in the book so far.

1. Write an ending for *Lord of the Flies,* picking up after Chapter 11 ends. Do not look ahead in the book while you do this.

Chapter 12

Cry of the Hunters

Journal and Discussion Topics

1. What do you think Ralph will be like when he grows up? Jack? Roger? Explain why you think as you do.
2. Why do you think Jack decided not to challenge Ralph when the officer asked who was the boss of the boys on the island?
3. Who is your favorite character? Explain your choice.
4. How did you expect the chase to end? How did you expect the book to end? What do you think of the actual ending?
5. How did the boys change from Chapter 1 to Chapter 12?
6. What were the boys' expectations for their island experience? Compare and contrast their expectations with the actual occurrences. Analyze how/why the differences occurred.
7. Do you share the vision of life that comes through *Lord of the Flies*? Explain how your vision is similar or how it differs?
8. Do you think this is a book you would ever reread? Why or why not?
9. How would you identify the protagonist and antagonist in this book? Explain your thinking.
10. Would you read another book by Golding? Explain your thinking.
11. How does Golding convey the emotions of fear/terror/horror?
12. What image from Chapter 12 struck you most deeply? Describe what you pictured in your mind's eye and explain why it resonated.
13. What examples of irony do you find in the final chapter?

Summary

Ralph lies in a covert for a long time. He realizes that he can't clean his wounds because in the water he could not hear the barefooted approach of the hunters. Bill comes by, and Ralph is struck by the separation between the boy, Bill, and the savage he sees. He approaches Castle Rock and sees that the watchman is being given meat. He concludes that he is safe for a brief time, and limps toward the fruit trees. As he walks, he tries at first to convince himself that the tribe will let him alone. But he knows from the deaths of Simon and Piggy that the tribe is descending further and further into savagery. He eats the fruit and wonders why two littluns scream and run at the sight of him. He goes toward the beach, but realizes that he can't spend the night there, and he moves back towards "Jack's end of the island." He comes again upon the sow's skull, and in rage and fear he hits it, knocking it from the stick to the ground where it breaks and lies grinning an even wider grin than when it was in one piece. He takes the stake on which it stood to use as a spear.

Ralph approaches Castle Rock. He hears the chant and knows the dance is in progress. He sees that Samneric are on guard, and this is a blow to him. Samneric have become savages like the rest. Piggy is dead. Ralph is alone. Nevertheless, he climbs up the rock to their perch and softly calls out to them. At first they are afraid, mistaking him for the beast. Then Sam, half-heartedly doing his duty, orders Ralph to leave. They reveal that they were tortured into joining the tribe. Ralph tries to find out what he's done to earn so much hatred, but they reply, "Never mind what's sense. That's gone." They warn him that the tribe is planning to "do him" the following day, throwing their spears at him, "Like at a pig." Ralph asks them what the tribe will do when they find him. Samneric don't answer, but urge him away. He asks them to come with him, but they are too afraid of Roger. They hear someone climbing towards them, and

Ralph hastily reveals his plan to lie close to the Castle Rock in a thicket, hoping that the tribe won't think of looking for him nearby and that Samneric can help keep the tribe from focusing on the spot. Sam shoves a chunk of meat into Ralph's hand, and even as he lowers himself, Ralph asks again, "What are you going to do—?" This time he receives an answer: Roger has sharpened a stick at both ends. Ralph cannot immediately make an association with this. He finds a place to hide, and begins to eat the meat, but he soon hears cries from Samneric, and realizes that one of them is in trouble.

He wakes to the ululation of the cordon beating the bushes for him. Soon after, he hears the interrogation of Samneric about his hiding place, and realizes that under torture they have revealed his secret. Still, he feels safe in his thicket, near the resting place of the rock that had hit Piggy. And then he hears the cry of "heave," and a large rock comes smashing through the thicket. The one that follows it knocks him in the air. A savage approaches and thrusts a pointed spear near Ralph, who strikes back, wounding the savage and revealing his location. Ralph waits, wondering what they are doing. He hears a rustling and sees smoke. Ralph scrambles out of the thicket, attacks the one savage he sees, and races through the undergrowth and a pig-run, hearing the cordon move up behind him. He tries to think of a plan and considers climbing a tree or breaking through the cordon. Then he wonders about hiding and letting them pass. He realizes that the tribe has set the island on fire and decides that hiding is better than a tree because if you're caught you have a better chance. He flings himself under a mat of vegetation and lies listening to the advancing fire, realizing that the fruit trees will be destroyed and they will have nothing left to eat. He continues his attempts to figure out the meaning of a stick sharpened at both ends, even as he realizes that he is holding one, but he still does not make the connection. An unidentified savage stoops to look under the mat and spots Ralph, Ralph bursts out of hiding, hits the savage with his stake, hears the others coming, and races away.

He passes a shelter as it bursts into flames, and he falls into the sand on the beach, rising to face a naval officer. The officer removes his hand from his revolver, and says "hullo." Ralph greets him in reply. The officer asks if there are any adults, and when Ralph shakes his head, responds, "fun and games." He grins cheerfully and says, "We saw your smoke." He asks if they've been having a war, and observing Ralph's nod, continues the game by asking "Any dead bodies?" Ralph says "only two." The littluns begin to appear, including Percival, who tries to recite his name and address, but can't remember them. The officer asks Ralph how many there are, but Ralph shakes his head. The officer asks who's boss, and Ralph speaks his answer, "I am." Jack starts to come forward, but stops and stands still. The officer chides them, saying British boys should have done better, and as Ralph tries to explain that things started off well, the officer mentions *Coral Island*. The reference recalls for Ralph all the hopes and dreams they'd had upon landing and the reality of Simon's death, and an unnamed thing that Jack had done. He begins to sob, weeping "for the end of innocence, the darkness of man's heart, and the fall through the air of the true, wise friend called Piggy." The other boys begin to cry, too. The officer turns and looks at his cruiser to give them time to recover.

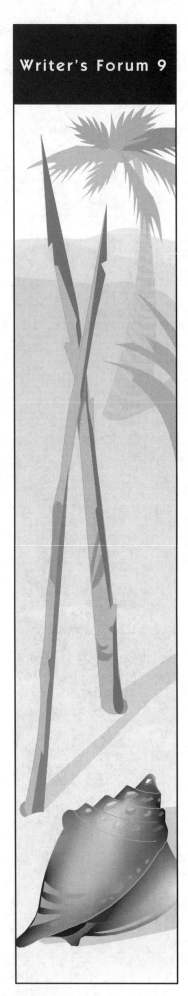

Writer's Forum 9 A News Article

A news article gives an objective report of an event that is important to the people who read that particular paper. While the event can be local, national, or international, it must have some impact on or hold some interest for the readership.

The headline of a news article both catches the reader's attention and declares the main topic of the article. Sports or feature articles may have a cryptic headline or one that includes wordplay to get the reader interested, but news headlines are usually straightforward.

The first paragraph of a news article gives the reader a quick summary of the important details, usually by telling the 5 W's (Who, What, Where, When, Why) and How. The following paragraphs give additional details that fill out the story.

News stories often include material gathered from interviews. This material may be stated indirectly or directly as quotations. If direct quotations are used, proper capitalization and punctuation should accompany it. Use care to make sure that you write the person's exact words. If you're not sure, ask.

1. Write a news story telling the world about the rescue of the boys from the island. You may make up supporting information to add details to the story. You may also decide when the story was released. The story should include an interview with at least one individual who was on the island.

   You may decide the readership of your paper. This will help shape how you choose to tell the story. Decide the name of the newspaper for which you are writing. Give yourself a byline, and make your story look like a news article. You may include an illustration with a caption if you wish.

Strategy 15

Consulting Outside References

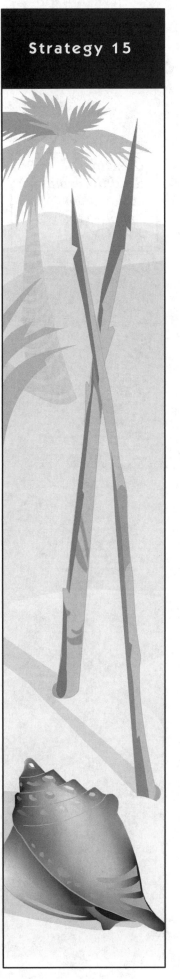

There are several different occasions on which you might want to consult a source beyond the novel itself.

FOLLOWING UP ALLUSIONS

If you want to understand as closely as possible what the boys would have been thinking when they shout the names of the adventures they hope to imitate, you should get copies of the books and read them.

R. L. Stevenson	*Treasure Island*	Puffin Books	1994
R. M. Ballantyne	*The Coral Island*	Puffin Books	1994 (abridged)
A. Ransome	*Swallows and Amazons*	Godine	1985

DOING RESEARCH

To understand *Lord of the Flies* from a critical perspective, you might want to read some of the published criticism. If you read it before you read the work itself, it will likely spoil the ending and interfere with your ability to form your own judgments, so it is recommended that you not read criticism until you have finished the work. Look at the bottom of the Bibliography List your teacher supplies to get you started. Also check out Amazon.com and barnesandnoble.com for lists of criticism. Then check the bibliographies in the critical works you read.

UNDERSTANDING SYMBOLS

If you want to understand more about the snake symbolism, for example, you might need to use some outside sources. The following are sources that are good for you to get to know:

The Bible (available in many versions and many languages; the version may matter, depending on your purpose).
Cruden's Concordance of the Holy Scriptures (helps you locate passages in the Bible that have a particular word in them).
The Herder Dictionary of Symbols: Symbols from Art, Archaeology, Mythology, Literature, and Religion, 1993, Chiron Publishing.

GENERAL SOURCES

Try *Britannica On-line, Encyclopaedia Britannica* or other on-line print encyclopedias for general information about things like:

- coral islands
- hunting and gathering
- South Seas
- atomic war
- William Golding

STRATEGY 16   Rereading a Book

Directions: Read the explanation, then complete the exercise.

Think of a book you've known for a while and have read at least twice. How does your understanding of this book differ from the way you understand a book you've read only once?

- Do you remember details better?
- Do you remember the sequence of events better?
- Have you memorized parts of it?
- Can you imagine the characters in another setting?
- Do you return to the book when you feel a certain way or want to feel a certain way?
- Do you feel that all the parts of the book fit together to form a whole integrated experience?

Authors and critics alike suggest that reading fiction should be experiential. Novelist Joseph Conrad wrote, "My task, which I am trying to achieve, is, by the power of the written word, to make you hear, to make you feel—it is before all, to make you see. That, and no more, but it is everything." Janet Burroway, a writing instructor elaborates: "Written words are . . . at two removes from experience. . . . They are transmitted first to the mind, where they must be translated into images. . . . What it means is that . . . [the] fiction writer [must] focus attention, not on the words, which are inert, nor on the thoughts these words produce, but through these to felt experience, where the vitality of understanding lies." In other words, we don't read literature for information; we read it in order to pass through (in our minds) the sequence of events the author proposes, allowing our minds and hearts to respond to these events.

But all of this doesn't happen without the extended and complex act that we call reading. And in our first reading of a text, we cannot give ourselves fully to experiencing the story because we have to:

- recognize black marks on the paper as letters and words
- process the words in groups to construct meaning and figure out how paragraphs and ideas are connected
- relate the perceived meaning to what we already know about stories in general, stories of the same genre as the one we're reading, earlier information from this particular story, etc.
- create in our minds the world of the story
- apply prior knowledge of facts, experiences, other stories, ideas, feelings, sensory data, etc. to help us understand what we have read
- try to recollect a new sequence of events and many facts and details
- fill gaps left by the text (no text tells absolutely everything that happened) with our own elaborations

Considering the enormous investment of energy required to read, author Vladimir Nabokov said, "one cannot *read* a book: one can only reread it. . . . When we read a book for the first time the very process of laboriously moving our eyes from left to right, line after line, page after page, this complicated physical work upon the book, the very process of learning in terms of space and time what the book is about, this stands between us and artistic appreciation. . . . In reading a book, we must have time to acquaint ourselves with it. We have no physical organ (as we have the eye in regard to a painting) that takes in the whole picture and then can enjoy its details. But at a second, or third, or fourth reading we do, in a sense, behave towards a book as we do towards a painting."

Rereading is also important when we want to clarify, re-experience, or check on our understanding of a link between different parts of a book.

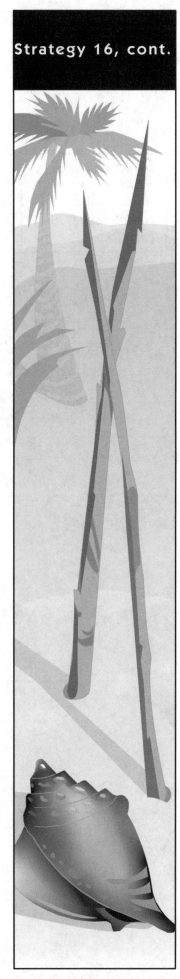

Think about the events of Chapter 12. As you were reading Samneric's answer to Ralph's question, "What are you going to do–?" (page 220), did you remember where you had read earlier in the book of a stick sharpened at both ends? Did you go back and find the place so you could reread and understand what fate awaited Ralph? This is the kind of situation in which rereading is important even before you've finished the story for the first time. The stick is a crucial element and "incomprehensible" to Ralph, but it shouldn't be to you. It was first mentioned in "Gift for the Darkness" (page 156) when Jack told Roger to sharpen a stick at both ends and then used the stick to impale the pig's head and create the Lord of the Flies. In order for you to understand the fate in store for Ralph, you need to know that they intend, not only to murder him, but to behead him and put his head on a stick. Your understanding depends on having the earlier passage in mind when you read.

1. Reread *Lord of the Flies*. Keep track of things that you notice in your second reading that you bypassed without paying attention the first time. Write a brief compare and contrast essay, to show the similarities and differences in the two readings.

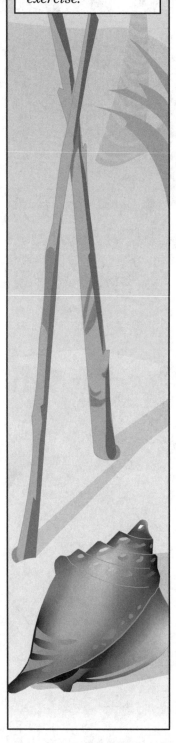

Directions: Read the explanation, then complete the exercise.

STRATEGY 17

The **theme** of a story might be thought of as the story's point or its message. A theme is usually a generalization about life or human behavior or values—true, but not a truism: the author's insight into the way things are that s/he wants to share with readers. Theme is an important part of a story's meaning and is developed throughout the story. And it is important to note that a story can have multiple themes and meanings.

A persuasive or didactic piece of writing (such as a fable) might have an explicit moral—a clear statement of theme. Such a statement can both clearly convey the author's idea of what the story means, while at the same time limiting interpretation of the piece on the part of the reader. However, a piece of writing that was written with experience or aesthetic response in mind is more open to interpretation. Certainly the author may have a theme or themes in mind, but the readers bring their own understandings, and in this case different readers may legitimately find different meanings based on patterns and messages in the text combined with their own interpretations and insights. But we seek for a balance between what is in the text and what the reader brings to the text. The message, however the reader interprets it, is always shaped by the author's intention and purpose.

Besides patterns in the story (which often point to the theme), there are certain parts of a story that often refer to the theme: the title, the beginning and the very end. An important character's first and final words or thoughts are also likely to carry powerful indications of theme.

In a story such as *Lord of the Flies*, which deals with complex issues, you will likely find multiple themes. But also try looking for a single, over-arching theme.

1. State the theme or themes you find as you review the novel in your mind. Explain how you concluded that these insights are thematic.

STRATEGY 18 — Comparing and Contrasting a Book and a Movie

Directions: Read the explanation, then complete the exercise.

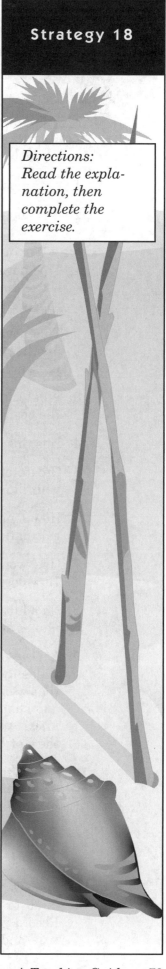

As you may recall from Writer's Forum 6 on a compare and contrast essay (page 57), in such an essay you show the similarities and differences between two or more people, things, ideas, approaches, etc., and draw some conclusions based on this examination. You choose the categories to compare and contrast based on your purpose, and these categories will change depending on your topic.

Sometimes, when considering literature, you will want to compare and contrast two different treatments of the same subject in different genres or media. You might want to do this if one work has been adapted or translated to create a new work, or if a work has inspired or influenced another work, or if they have the same subject and enough in common or such wide differences that you think it would be fruitful to see the similarities and differences in how they make meaning and achieve their effects.

In this particular case, you are going to contrast the book *Lord of the Flies* with one or both of the two movies based on the book. Usually it is easier to do this if you both read the book twice and watch a movie at least twice, once to experience it, and once to take notes for your paper. Here are some questions that it would be useful to examine:

- Did the theme(s) you identified in the book come out in the movie? If not, what message(s) did the movie give?
- A movie is usually no longer than 2 hours, so a movie adaptation of a full-length book always leaves out material included in the book. What is excerpted or compressed in this movie?
- A movie script may have additional material not included in the book, or may make changes in the book. What additions and/or changes do you notice?
- How did your mental images of the characters, settings, and actions of the book differ from the way they were presented in the movie? Compare the characterizations and the plots carefully.
- Apart from the book, did the movie work as an experience in itself? Did it hold your interest? Was it worthwhile?
- Did the theme(s) you identified in the book come out in the movie? If not, what message(s) did the movie give?
- Which did you like better—the book or the movie? Why?

Words that can help you express concepts of similarity and difference include the following:

SIMILARITY

- as well as
- similarly
- likewise
- alike
- at the same time
- resemble

DIFFERENCE

- differ
- whereas
- however
- while
- but
- on the contrary
- conversely
- though
- on the other hand

1. Write an essay comparing and contrasting the book and one of the two movies of *Lord of the Flies* (Peter Brook, 1963, or Harry Hook, 1990.)

Vocabulary

Look at each group of words. Tell why it is important in the story.

1. antiphonal, ululation _____

2. drill, epaulettes _____

Essay Topics

1. This novel is set on a deserted tropical island. Think of another story you know that is set on an island. Describe the similarities and differences in the two settings and the role of setting in each story.

2. This novel could be described as a "coming of age" story. Compare and contrast it with another "coming of age" story. What views of adulthood and childhood does each story present?

3. What connections do you find between the occurrences in the adult world referred to at the beginning and end of the book and the boys' experiences on the island?

4. Has this book changed any of your fundamental ideas? Explain your thinking.

5. Create an illustration for your favorite part of the book. Write an explanation of how your illustration depicts the portion of text you have chosen.

6. How long has passed since the boys landed on the island? How did you make your calculation?

7. How would the book be different if Golding ended with the description of Ralph's grief? How does the final paragraph shape the book?

8. No adult in this book is referred to by name. What does this convey to you? What other names are missing from the book? Why do you think Golding omitted them?

9. A *Deus ex machina* is an unexpected and nearly miraculous shift of events that suddenly resolves the action of a plot. The name comes from a piece of stage machinery that was used to lower a god or goddess from "the heavens" to intervene in the action and shape the ending of a Greek play. What do you think of the ending of *Lord of the Flies*? Were you surprised? Was it believable to you? Do you think it fits the world of the story that Golding created?

10. Project the ending of the book into the future. Write on one of the following topics:
    a the first meeting of one of the boys with his family
    b. the first day of school
    c. a meeting at the dock with a news reporter
    d. the debriefing on board ship by the ship's officer
    e. Jack's and Ralph's first private face-to-face meeting on board ship

11. Simon's prophetic statement that Ralph would go home proved true. Return in your mind to what you thought about Simon's statement to Ralph when you first read it. Record your re-analysis of Simon's character now that you know that his prophecy was true, and tell what you think his presence in the book means.

HISTORY OF IDEAS

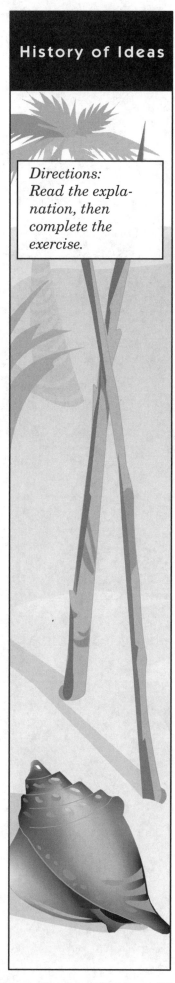

Directions: Read the explanation, then complete the exercise.

INTRODUCTION

The term **history of ideas** refers to part of what makes up our social and historical context—the ongoing give and take across time and across cultures about important issues in our world. The best political system; the appropriate means and ends of education; the nature of human beings; the role of human beings in the natural world; whether God exists and if so, how human beings can relate to God; the definition of culture; and whether or not war is ever justified are some of the important topics that have been argued and debated across the centuries.

Every artist lives in a social and historical context. Writers incorporate the issues, ideas, and popular culture of their day in a variety of ways in their works. It can be helpful to the understanding of a work of literature to know more about the author's context—more about what the writer takes for granted, what he or she is moving toward, and what he or she eschews.

The following pages will give you an introduction to some of the ideas that shaped the debate into which Golding entered with his book. But please be aware that they necessarily simplify the doctrines and ideas they express, and if you want to *really* understand a person's thoughts and ideas, you should study the person's own expression of them.

HUMAN NATURE

Golding said in the publicity questionnaire about *Lord of the Flies* that "the theme is an attempt to trace the defects of society back to the defects of human nature." Where does this fit in the history of ideas about human nature? One answer might be "directly opposite the Swiss-French thinker and writer Jean-Jacques Rousseau." Born in Geneva in 1712, Rousseau was the seminal thinker in the movement called **naturalism**, which grows out of his idea that human beings are naturally good and innocent.

1. If you were arguing that Golding disagrees with Rousseau about human nature, what portions of *Lord of the Flies* would you cite as evidence? Is there any evidence to show agreement between Golding and Rousseau?

Golding's view of human nature has resonances with the Christian doctrine of **Original Sin.** This is a descriptive doctrine, based in the Bible and addressing the nature of people. It says that everyone is born with the disposition to sin, that is, that we are not innocents at birth who are corrupted by life. One difference between Golding's view and the Christian doctrine is that Christianity presents a remedy for man's sinful nature—the possibility of salvation through Jesus Christ.

2. Samuel Hynes in his essay "William Golding's *Lord of the Flies*" (1968) says, "The novel tells us a good deal about evil; but about salvation it is silent." Do you find any hope for salvation in the novel, any hint that there could be change or improvement in the lot of human beings? Explain.

CIVILIZATION/CULTURE

According to the American Heritage dictionary, a **culture** is "The behavior patterns, arts, beliefs, institutions, and all other products of human work and thought, especially as expressed in a particular community or period." The parts of a culture are not distinct and separated, but rather are integrated, and in-

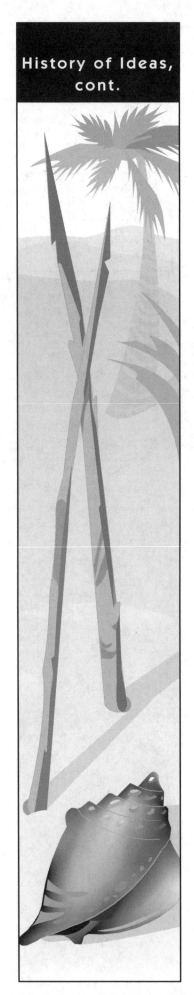

clude such elements as language, ideas, beliefs, institutions, customs, taboos, rituals, and works of art.

Cultures arise from primitive hunting and gathering societies. Agriculture and domestication of animals seem to be key factors in moving toward culture and civilization because a steady food supply allows for permanent settlement, which in turn leads to specialization of jobs and eventually, leisure time. Yet, human beings born into a culture are born without culture. The process of education is what "enculturates" them.

3. Using the elements of culture listed above, compare and contrast the culture on the island with the culture the boys left at home, as revealed by hints in the text. What elements of culture are the boys lacking on the island?

4. Is there enculturation on the island, and if so, how does it work?

A corollary to Rousseau's belief about people's natural innocence is that people become corrupted by living in society and civilization, which were not originally bad in themselves but became harmful as they became sophisticated. Rousseau believed that people's passions (strong feelings such as anger) were naturally dormant, but roused by living in society. Rousseau also felt strongly that property was a chief cause of the degeneration of human beings from their pure natural state.

But the concept of culture includes the inherent suggestion that **society**—contrary to Rousseau's view—raises humans toward perfection and rationality from ignorance and a reign of the passions. James Henry Breasted said, "The fact that man possessed the capacity to rise from bestial savagery to civilization . . . is the greatest fact in the history of the universe known to us." But this does not suggest that it is even difficult, let alone impossible, for humankind to regress: "You think that a wall as solid as the earth separates civilization from barbarism. I tell you the division is a thread, a sheet of glass. A touch here, a push there, and you bring back the reign of Saturn," said Sir John Buchan.

5. From evidence in *Lord of the Flies*, would you say that Golding would have agreed or disagreed with the statement that "society perfects people"? With the statement that "society corrupts people"? Explain.

Civilization is an advanced state of cultural development and carries with it certain behavioral norms. Behavior that falls outside of the normal or accepted limits for Western culture has sometimes been called **savage** by Westerners. The term has also been used to describe people of cultures with different moral or social norms than those of Westerners. Thus the word *savage* has connotations of practice of polytheism or of a religion other than Christianity, lack of restraint, immorality, injustice, and violence.

6. The boys in *Lord of the Flies* start off believing that they cannot be savages because they are British. But some of them question this stance before the novel is over. One of the distinguishing characteristics of the civilized person is the observation of laws, rules, and taboos (the avoidance of certain activities or behaviors). The boys on the island violate some basic laws, rules, and taboos of their home culture, particularly when they are wearing paint. Do you think it is justified to say that they have regressed to savagery? What are your criteria?

GOVERNMENT

The Greek philosopher Plato categorized forms of government in a schema that is still referred to today. He believed that democracy (government by the many) inevitably degenerates into a lawless anarchy, followed by a tyranny.

7. Does *Lord of the Flies* show this progression? Explain your thinking.

German sociologist Max Weber proposed a schema of government with three basic types of rule: **charismatic,** in which authority is based on faith in a particular leader and his/her gifts; **traditional,** in which authority is transmitted in a set manner, like a hereditary monarchy; and **rational-legal**, in which the government proceeds out of a legal order.

8. How could categorizing Ralph's and Jack's governments both as "charismatic," rather than (for example) as a democracy and a tyranny, shed light on their rises to and falls from power?

9. Piggy had an important role in Ralph's government and Roger in Jack's, but neither was ever given a title or specific designation. If Ralph and Jack had offices in government today, what titles would Piggy and Ralph have held? Explain your reasoning.

VIOLENCE/WAR

Some of the first violence in the novel is manifested around the hunt for pigs. Some people are opposed to using animals for food. Mahatma Gandhi said, "I do not regard flesh-food as necessary for us at any stage and under any clime in which it is possible for human beings ordinarily to live." Golding shows the boys moving from a vegetarian diet to a diet that includes pork.

10. As you read about killing the pigs, did you think that Golding was opposed on principle to the use of animals for food? Explain how you understood it.

Some theorists view war as due to human biology and psychology: we are aggressive creatures to whom violence is not unnatural. For example, Konrad Lorenz (1903-1989), the founder of ethology, concluded from his research that humans have instinctive aggressions.

Others see war as the result of society—a result of faulty institutions or problematic social relations. John Stuart Mill (1806–1873), a British social and political thinker, concluded that wars result from autocratic governments, ignoring the will of their peaceful populace. German economist and revolutionist Karl Marx (1818–1883) thought that war was due to class structure and was necessary to overthrow imperialist and capitalist governments.

Some see war as a rational approach for achieving certain political goals. Prussian general Carl Philipp Gottfried von Clausewitz (1780–1831) considered war as a practical extension of policy, the application of force for political ends.

Still others thought war was an inevitable element of human evolution. Georg Hegel (1770–1831), a German philosopher, was of the opinion that conflict is necessary to progress, with war being the supreme example of conflict.

11. An anarchist named Emma Goldman said, "It is organized violence on top which creates individual violence at the bottom." Do you think that *Lord of the Flies* demonstrates this? Explain. Do you yourself believe it? Explain. In your answers, explain to the best of your ability what Golding and you respectively each think causes war.

12. Author William Allen White said, "There is no such thing as civilized warfare." Do you think Golding would agree? Why or why not? Do you agree? Why or why not?

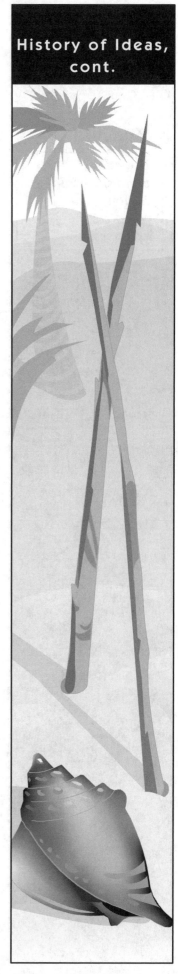

Theme Page
Friendship and Loyalty

Directions:
Read the explanation, then complete the exercises.

Friendship is one of the intimate kinds of human relationships, often between just two people. Golding features several close pairs in this book:
- Ralph and Piggy
- Jack and Roger
- Samneric

1. People have differing definitions of friendship. What's your definition? What's the difference between friends and other kinds of partnerships? Consider the quotations below in framing your response.

   - "A Friend Is Someone Who Likes You" (book title)

   - "A friend knows the song in your heart and can sing it back to you when you have forgotten how it goes." —Quoted by Robert J. Wicks in *Living a Gentler, Passionate Life*

   - "It is one of the severest tests of friendship to tell your friend his faults. So to love a man that you cannot bear to see a stain upon him, and to speak painful truth through loving words, that is friendship." —Henry Ward Beecher

   - "Kindred weaknesses induce friendships as often as kindred virtues." —Christian Nestell Bovee

   - "True friendship is an identity of souls rarely to be found in this world. Only between like natures can friendship be altogether worthy and enduring." —Mahatma Gandhi

2. Joseph Addison, British author, said "Without constancy there is neither love, friendship, nor virtue in the world." How does loyalty figure in *Lord of the Flies* both in friendship and in other contexts?

3. Which of Golding's pairs listed above do you think are friends? Explain.

4. How do you think Golding would define friendship? What do you think he would say about each pair listed above?

SAVE THIS QUESTION UNTIL STUDENTS HAVE FINISHED READING:

5. What do you think is the significance of friendship in the book? In your answer, consider what would have happened to Ralph without Piggy? To Jack without Roger? To Sam or Eric without the other? Also consider your own reaction to the changes in Jack, to Piggy's death, and to Ralph's grief.

Theme Page

People and Nature

Directions: Read the explanation, then complete the exercises.

We frequently consider the interaction of people and nature when we think about setting. We talk about setting as an assistant or an obstacle in the protagonist's attempt to reach a goal; we talk about setting as creating mood; we observe how a character's preference for a particular setting can reveal his or her personality. In this book, the interactions between people and nature are particularly complex.

1. Can nature be said to be benevolent or malevolent, or is it both or neither? Explain your answer. How do you react to the following quotation from Ralph Waldo Emerson?

   "Nature is no sentimentalist—does not cosset or pamper us. We must see that the world is rough and surly, and will not mind drowning a man or a woman, but swallows your ships like a grain of dust. The cold, inconsiderate of persons, tingles your blood, benumbs your feet, freezes a man like an apple. The diseases, the elements, fortune, gravity, lightning, respect no persons."

2. What kind of interactions do the boys have with nature? Do these types of interactions change through the book? Do the interactions assist or impede their goals; create mood; or reveal character? What do you think they mean?

3. How do the boys feel about nature? Do their feelings change through the book?

4. What are the ways that Golding uses nature to create meaning for the reader of the narrative?

SAVE THE FOLLOWING TWO QUESTIONS UNTIL STUDENTS HAVE FINISHED READING:

5. The first interaction between people and nature in the events of the book is the landing of the boys on the island. The last implied interaction is their departure, which is not narrated. How does Golding present the first interaction? Imagine that the boys have left. How is the island different as a result of their presence?

6. Imagine that you are an anthropologist and you arrived on the island a week after the boys left, but without any knowledge of their stay. What conclusions might you draw from the evidence you would find?

Theme Page Leadership and Authority

Directions: Read the explanation, then complete the exercises.

Golding raises many questions about authority and leadership in this novel. He shows young men separated from the world of adult authority, trying to work out their own systems of government, authority, and power.

1. In your opinion, what should be the relationship between authority and office? Between authority and character? What qualities make a good leader?

SAVE THE FOLLOWING QUESTIONS UNTIL STUDENTS HAVE FINISHED READING:

2. What/who are the authorities in this narrative? What powers do the boys pay heed to? What does each authority stand for? For each of the characters listed, tell what you think he considered the greatest authority in his life: Ralph, Piggy, Simon, Jack, Roger, the officer?

3. Which of the authorities presented in this book were legitimate or deserving of respect and obedience and which weren't, in your opinion? Which had the greatest power?

4. How were the authorities represented in the book invested with power or how did they acquire it?

5. By what means did the authorities keep their power? Which authorities do you judge to have lost their power? Explain your response.

6. It could be said that Ralph's government and his leadership failed. Explain how this failure came about and what factors you think contributed to this failure. Consider the following quotation.

"Society cannot exist unless a controlling power upon will and appetite be placed somewhere; and the less of it there is within, the more there must be without. It is ordained in the eternal constitution of things, that men of intemperate minds cannot be free. Their passions forge their fetters." Edmund Burke

7. John Mason Brown said, "Politics, . . . is a realm peopled only by villains or heroes, in which everything is black or white and gray is a forbidden color." What color would you consider each of the various authorities in this book? Explain why.

8. Now that you're done with the novel, what do you think Golding is saying about the nature of power and authority? About the qualities of good leadership?

9. How would you apply these quotations to the novel:

"Power acquired by guilt has seldom been directed to any good end or useful purpose." —Tacitus

"All power is a trust." —Benjamin Disraeli

10. If you had been Piggy, would you have stayed loyal to Ralph, even when his leadership faltered? Explain.

Theme Page   Maturity and Adulthood

Directions: Read the explanation, then complete the exercises.

By showing a group of young men removed from the context of adult society, Golding calls into question the meaning of adulthood and maturity and the role of education.

1. What do you think is the difference between being a young man and a man? A young woman and a woman?

2. Adulthood is partially defined in our society by law. At age 16 or so, one is able to earn a driver's license. Then, at age 18 one can vote, and at 21 one gains other privileges. How would you define an "adult"?

3. Would you consider adulthood different from maturity? How would you explain the relationship?

4. What is education? What is it's purpose? Does education in a democracy have particular requirements that are different from education in a society that is not democratic? How does education relate to adulthood and maturity? Consider these quotations:

   • "I have never let my schooling interfere with my education."
     —Mark Twain

   • "Education comes to us from nature, men, or things. The inward development of our faculties and organs is the education of nature; the use which we are taught to make of this development is the education of men; and what we gain from our own experience of the objects around us is the education of things." —Jean Jacques Rousseau

   • "Not education, but character, is man's greatest need and man's greatest safeguard." —Herbert Spencer

5. From the implicit and explicit details in the text, put together a description of the education the boys on the island were receiving at their schools at home. Do you think Golding approves of the education the boys on the island had received? Explain.

6. Do you think that a different kind of education in school would have better prepared the boys for life on the island? Explain. Do you think that kind of preparation should be included in everyone's education? Explain.

7. Piggy, in disgust, often calls the others "a crowd of kids." How would you describe Piggy's concept of adulthood? Do you think his criticism of the others is just? Explain.

SAVE THE FOLLOWING TWO QUESTIONS UNTIL STUDENTS HAVE FINISHED READING:

8. What did the boys (Ralph, Piggy, Simon, and Jack particularly) learn while on the island? What relationship do you imagine their learning might have with Ralph's and Jack's lives when they return home?

9. What did you learn from this book? Has the experience of reading and thinking about *Lord of the Flies* contributed to your education? To your becoming a mature individual? To your becoming an adult? Explain how.

Theme Page   Status and Reputation

Golding presents a group of young men, many of whom don't know each other, brought together in an unusual situation. Very quickly, status and repu-tation become important and a hierarchy develops.

1. How important are status and reputation in the world? How can a good reputation be a benefit to an individual or to society as a whole? How important are status and reputation in your life? Do you think your reputation reflects your true character? If there is a difference, how do you account for it?

2. Are hierarchies necessary in society? In work? In family life? How are these three situations similar and how are they different? Explain your thinking.

3. Explain the hierarchies at work on the island. How did they change over time? What were the most influential factors in forming the hierarchies?

4. What gave Ralph status in the community at the beginning of the story? How and why did Ralph's status in the community change? What gave Jack status at the beginning? How and why did Jack's status in the community change?

5. Piggy clearly had an important role in Ralph's government. In your opinion, if Piggy had challenged Ralph for a leadership role, could he have gained one? Explain your thinking. Roger had an important role in Jack's government. In your opinion, if Roger had challenged Jack for a leadership role, what would have happened? Explain your thinking.

6. Edgar Watson Howe, an American editor and author, said, "What people say behind your back is your standing in the community in which you live." Which characters in the book are talked about behind their backs? What kinds of things are said about them? How did this affect their standing in the community?

7. Henry Ward Beecher said, "A man's character is the reality of himself. His reputation is the opinion others have formed of him. Character is in him;—reputation is from other people—that is the substance, this is the shadow." Which character(s) in *Lord of the Flies* do you think live with a great difference between their character and the public estimation of it? What explanation can you offer for this divergence? Which characters, if any, are judged accurately by their peers, in your opinion? Explain. Did your judgments of characters as you read rely on their character or on their reputation or the separation between the two? Explain.

SAVE THE FOLLOWING TWO QUESTIONS UNTIL STUDENTS HAVE FINISHED READING:

8. In the end, which do you think had more influence on the community: Piggy's character and reputation or Roger's character and reputation? Explain your thinking. How did each of them influence Ralph?

9. Simon foresaw that Ralph would have the opportunity to leave the island. Simon's experience with the Lord of the Flies led him to a deep understanding of human nature. Why do you think Simon didn't have more status and influence among his peers?

Theme Page   Memory and Forgetting

Theme Page

Directions: Read the explanation, then complete the exercises.

What people remember and what they forget can be significant. Golding makes a point of what is remembered and what is forgotten by the boys on the island.

1. What importance do personal memories have? Why is remembering certain facts important? What kinds of memories are important to society? Why?

2. Is forgetfulness good, bad, neutral, or does it depend? What kinds of situations and events can cause or encourage forgetfulness? Explain your thinking. Consider these quotations:

   "What's too painful to remember, we simply choose to forget." —from the song "The Way We Were"

   "There is a noble forgetfulness—that which does not remember injuries." —Charles Simmons

   "A little neglect may breed great mischief: for want of a nail the shoe was lost; for want of a shoe the horse was lost, and for want of a horse the rider was lost, being overtaken and slain by an enemy, all for want of a little care about a horse-shoe nail." —Benjamin Franklin

3. What is your understanding of the significance of forgetfulness in the novel? Consider the meaning of these events in the book:

   • Ralph's forgetting the purpose of the fire
   • Jack's hunters forgetting to tend the fire
   • The older boys forgetting about the littluns during the first fire
   • Ralph purposely trying to forget the boy with the birthmark (Chapter 5)
   • Percival Wemys Madison forgetting his name and address (Chapter 12)
   • The boys forgetting about/neglecting to wash and clean themselves

4. What is your understanding of the significance of memory in the novel? Consider the meaning of the these events in the book:

   • The older boys' remembrance of books about deserted islands: *Treasure Island, Swallows and Amazons,* and *Coral Island* (Chapter 2)

   • Piggy's remembering and reminding Ralph of the purpose of the fire

   • Percival Wemys Madison remembering and reciting his name and address

   • The boys (particularly Piggy) remembering and reenacting rules and standards from home

   • Piggy remembering and naming the two dead boys and calling Simon's death "murder" (Chapter 12)

5. What is the relationship between writing and memory? How do oral societies preserve memories? What effects do you think resulted from the transfer of the young men in the novel from a literate to an oral society?

Theme Page   Reality and Responsibility

*Directions:
Read the expla-
nation, then
complete the
exercises.*

It might be said that the boys enter into their island experience in the spirit of adventure and play. But soon they have started a fire that results in at least one death and they do not even know how many more of the littluns might have been lost. Golding presents a group of young men suddenly faced with reality and responsibility.

1. We usually consider play the realm of children, and reality something that people deal with more and more as they become adults. In what ways do play and reality differ?

2. What do you think it means to be responsible? How do you know when something is your responsibility?

3. There are several references to play in the story (for example, pages 145, 205, and 233). Explain their significance.

4. One of the realities the boys on the island face is that they are in a place with no adults. What do you think of their various reactions to that reality?

SAVE THE FOLLOWING QUESTIONS UNTIL STUDENTS HAVE FINISHED READING:

5. In what ways do the older boys try to take responsibility for the littluns? In your opinion, in what ways do the older boys fail in taking responsibility for the littluns?

6. How do the boys deal with the responsibility for the different deaths that occur while they are on the island? How are the responses to the different deaths different? How are they similar?

7. If a classmate or neighbor of the boys had died from an illness at home in England, what would likely have happened? If a classmate or neighbor had died at home from the same causes as the boy with the birthmark or Simon or Piggy, what would likely have happened? Why do you think the boys don't create a court as part of their island government?

8. How are guilt and dereliction of duty dealt with in our society and religious communities? Would the boys on the island have been better off, in your opinion, if there had been some kind of consequences for their failures? Explain your answer.

9. As Golding presents it, might a different group of boys with different virtues have fared better on the island, creating an orderly society in which no citizen came to harm? Explain your thinking. Do you agree with what you take to be Golding's assessment? Why or why not? Include a reaction to the following quotation from Golding in your answer: "The theme [of *Lord of the Flies*] is an attempt to trace the defects of society back to the defects of human nature. The moral is that the shape of a society must depend on the ethical nature of the individual and not on any political system however apparently logical or respectable."

Theme Page

Fear

Directions: Read the explanation, then complete the exercises.

Fear is both universal and individual. Every person experiences fear, but some fear arises from things that scare nearly everyone, for example, pain and death, while some of the objects of fear are idiosyncratic. Fear is an important force in the plot of *Lord of the Flies.*

1. Some fears arise from things that are known. Some arise from things that are unknown. How do you think these two kinds of fear influence people?

2. Sometimes fears can be overcome. What do you think are useful approaches to dealing with fear?

SAVE THE FOLLOWING QUESTIONS UNTIL STUDENTS HAVE FINISED READING

3. Some fears come from imaginary dangers. Other fears are responses to real dangers. How would you assess the fears that arise in the course of the plot of the novel?

4. Discuss how each of the fears listed below fits into the plot. How did each one influence the boys' decisions and actions?

   • Fear of "the beast"
   • Fear of pain
   • Fear of death
   • Fear of not being rescued
   • Fear of being unable to see
   • Fear of hunger

5. Discuss the following quotations in relation to the novel:

   • "Often the fear of one evil leads us into a worse."
   —Nicolas Boileau-Despréaux

   • "There are very few monsters that warrant the fear we have of them."
   —André Gide

   • "We must face what we fear; that is the case of the core of the restoration of health." —Max Lerner

   • "Fear often produces cruelty and frightfulness." —Jawaharlal Nehru

6. From Golding's perspective, what would you say was the most fearful thing on the island? Explain your thoughts. What is your response to what you understand to be Golding's assessment?

Strategy 1: Beginning a Book, page 16

1. Answers will vary. Students may find the title cryptic. A few may catch the allusion to Beelzebub.
2. Answers will vary. Students may guess that power and governance may be involved. Some may interpret the flies as a symbol of decay because flies buzz around garbage and carrion. Students who understand the reference to Beelzebub may think that the book will be about evil.
3. Answers will vary depending on the edition used.
4. The book was originally published in Great Britain in 1954.
5. Answers will vary.
6. Pulitzer Prize in 1983; Possible response: it shows a high level of accomplishment in literature.
7. Possible response: Ralph seems like a sterotyped jock: athletic, good-looking, careless of other people's feelings, not wanting things to be too serious, but not a bad person. Piggy is lower-class, and his fatness, asthma, nearsightedness, and bad grammar make him seem like someone to avoid, but he seems to be thoughtful and practical and sensitive.
8. Possible response: Ralph, Piggy and other children were evacuated from England by plane. The airport was later hit by an atom bomb. During the flight, the plane was attacked and destroyed except for the passenger cabin in which the children were riding which landed on what seems to be a tropical island. The cabin has been pulled out to sea now, apparently with some children still in it. It seems that there are likely to be some other children on the island. The only food source Piggy has found gives him diarrhea. There are no adults on the island, and no adult anywhere in the world knows where they are.
9. Students may mention that the narration seems to be third-person omniscient (see Strategy 9). The narrator describes the setting in detail, but often doesn't identify the speaker in the dialogue, although it's possible to figure out who's talking. The narrator tells what is going on in both Ralph's and Piggy's minds. Since the narration seems straightforward and objective, students are likely to trust it.
10. Ralph and Piggy are the only characters presented so far, and both seem important.
11. The story is set on what seems to be an island in a tropical climate. Most students will be unable to say for sure if the setting is real or imaginary. It is described realistically and in great detail, if imaginatively and using figurative language. As special characteristics, students might note: the apparent remoteness from anything else; the climate, which includes intense heat, sunshine, but also storms; the thorns and undergrowth; the fruit and coconuts that can be used for food.
12. Possible response: So far it seems to be a cross between several different genres: realistic fiction, adventure story, and desert island romance.
13. Possible response: The predicament of being marooned and trying to survive and be rescued.
14. Answers will vary, partly depending on how students interpret the genre. Possible response: Ralph and Piggy will locate some other children, and they will explore and make a plan for survival.
15. Possible responses: Are they really on an island? Is there any other food source that they can use? Is there fresh water? Is there a place they can take shelter from storms like the one that dragged the cabin out to sea? Where exactly is the island? Will Ralph realize that the situation is serious? Will Ralph listen to Piggy's ideas about organization?

Chapter 1: The Sound of the Shell, page 18

1. Possible response: While not as disdainful as Jack, Ralph clearly holds Piggy in low regard. Piggy respects Ralph and sees in him the popular fellow that Piggy wishes he could be. He gives Ralph credit for more than his due.

2. Answers will vary. Students may see the potential for: violence in Jack, conflict between Jack and Piggy and possibly between Jack and Ralph, the potential for Piggy being ostracized by the whole group, the potential for Ralph to be a failure as a leader because he isn't practical and has a tendency to prefer fantasy to reality.

3. Possible responses: Ralph stands on his head, tries to evade Piggy, swims really well (a talent that might be useful in this setting), makes fun of Piggy by using his nickname, and fantasizes—seems like he'll be popular but maybe ineffective. Piggy gets stuck with thorns, reasons out the situation (a very useful trait indeed), has diarrhea twice, and proposes counting and listing the group on the island—seems like he'll be unpopular but best thinker in the group. Jack has the choir members march in their black cloaks in the heat, asserts his right to be chief based on his ability to sing C sharp (which is absolutely irrelevant to their situation), throws a sheath-knife into a tree trunk to get the boys to be quiet—seems like he rules by threat and could be a trouble-maker. Roger avoids people and tries to stay secret; he also proposed the vote for chief—unknown quantity. Simon faints and sees the resemblance between the evergreen buds and candles—could be the "poet type" in the group.

4. Students may mention the British English (such as *garter*, *togs*, etc.); Piggy's grammatical errors—shows that Piggy's lower-class; Ralph's mispronunciation of *asthma*—shows that he's insensitive; the adjective *skull-like* and the word *snake-clasp* in the description involving Ralph at the top of page 5—may be reflecting hidden evil; the slang "You can't half swim," meaning, "You can swim really well"—slang makes it seem realistic; the words *Gib* (for Gibraltar) and *Addis* (for Addis Ababa) shows that the evacuation has taken the boys to northern Africa and indicates the extent of the war; Jack's insistence on using his last name, which only lasts from page 17 to page 18, where he is once "Jack Merridew" and then becomes "Jack"—his claim to superiority and maturity is made to seem unjustified.

5. Students may note, first of all, that it is all male and consists of boys between about 6 and thirteen or fourteen. Other possible responses: that there are already friendships, but also factions; that the so-called unity derived from making fun of Piggy is not a good sign; that Jack's high-handedness violates the ground rules of civility, let alone community; that the choir has special status; that the leader is not the person with the clearest and most practical ideas; that individual talent does not seem as important as charisma; that the older boys have taken charge, but have not given much thought yet to the younger boys,

6. The mystique of the conch, Ralph's personal appearance, and his stillness.

7. Possible responses: there is the possibility of a food source other than the fruit, so long as they can make a fire, but to make use of it, the boys are going to have to learn to kill—since the boys are in this predicament because of a war, this may indicate that violence is going to be an important theme in the book; Jack seems a little out of control and easily humiliated already—the appointment of him as a hunter seems like it could set the stage for an increase in his violent behavior.

8. Students may think that as long as Piggy sticks with Ralph to do the thinking, and if Ralph can keep Jack under control, he will do all right. Otherwise, they may imagine that things will deteriorate fairly quickly.

9. There is the choir; there is Jack/Ralph/Simon; there are the "small boys" (page 19); there is Piggy as odd-man-out.

Strategy 2: Plot—The Design of a Story, page 19

1. Students may identify the complication as beginning at the end of Chapter Two with the failure of the fire and the realization of the death of the boy with the birthmark. Because the boys are saved by a Deus ex Machina responding to a fire intended to flush Ralph out of the jungle so that he could be murdered, not intended to signal passing ships, and certainly not by Ralph's design, students may be unable to assign a crisis. The climax comes with the arrival of the officer. The resolution assures the boys' rescue, but is inconclusive in many ways. What is the situation to which they will be returned? How can they deal with what they've experienced? Etc.

Strategy 3: Forming Hypotheses, page 21

1. Answers will vary. Students should mention the beauty of the island and the virtues extolled by the boys. Among elements that might suggest foreboding, they might mention the "witch-like cry" of the bird (page 1), the thorns (page 1), the diarrhea caused by the fruit (page 4), the "torn" landscape with "fallen trees" and "decaying coconuts" (page 4), the "skull-like" shape of the coconuts (page 5), etc. They should end up with an entry for each chapter.

Strategy 4: Characterization, page 22

1. See answer to Chapter 1, Question 3.
2. Students may note the cruelty of the boys, Piggy's good-naturedness and strong desire for community, the comparison of Piggy and Fatty, as well as their own feelings about names and nicknames.
3. Students should note the communion that develops between Jack, Ralph, and Simon while they're exploring the island, and Simon's silence during the episode with the pig at the end of Chapter 1.
4. See answer to Chapter 1, Question 3.
5. Answers will vary. Students may say that Ralph treats Jack like an equal and Piggy like an inferior. He downplays Jack's failings and exaggerates Piggy's differences.
6. Ralph's response is purely practical: "you can't light them." Jack's combines the practical ("We can't eat them") with the destructive slashing at the tree, which is his first reaction. Simon enjoys trying to name the tree and the buds which resemble candles. He appreciates it for its beauty.

Writer's Forum 1: Description, page 23

1. Students may describe the beach in realistic or idyllic terms. They may choose to use the suggested categories for describing Ralph, Jack, or Piggy. They should include a description of their choice's language as well. Their reflections should touch on the difference between a physical description and a description of qualities, such as personality, that are invisible.

Chapter 2: Fire on the Mountain, page 24

1. Points to touch on include the choir becoming less of an exclusive group, the unified feeling that Ralph, Simon, and Jack have coming down from the mountain, the break-up of that unity in the meeting, the break-up of the meeting by the mad dash to build a fire, the commandeering of Piggy's glasses, Jack's change of rules—that the conch doesn't count on top of the mountain, the loss of the boy with the birthmark.
2. Students should mention Piggy's admonitions to the group to not hinder Ralph, his reasonable assessment of their true situation—that nobody knows where they are, his assistance to the boy with the mulberry-colored birthmark, his care of the conch, his admonitions to the group on the mountain top to plan and think and to watch out for the little 'uns, his recognition that there is a missing child.

3. Most students will agree that Ralph has not shown evidence of the reasoning ability and assessment of reality that would lead him to make such a statement.

4. Students should note Ralph's encouragement of the boy to come speak; Ralph's laughing at the boy; his kind (but perhaps untrue) explanation about the natural habitat of a "snake-thing"; his denial of the boy's experience with "rational assurance" that has no backing; and Ralph's growing exasperation and insistence to the point of almost yelling, so that at last the boy's claim is overcome by repetition, volume, and a change of subject rather than by truly convincing him that he's mistaken; the lack of personal concern and action to deal with the boy's fear and anxiety. Ralph seemed more concerned with the effect of the discussion on the others at the meeting than with quelling the boy's terror and finding out the truth.

5. Answers will vary. Accept reasonable responses based on the description in the text.

6. The goals are to have fun and be rescued. Students may think that being rescued is highly unlikely and that they should devote their attentions to creating a life for themselves on the island. They may agree with Piggy that the best approach would have been to start by making shelters rather than running off in a madcap and disorganized fashion and starting a fire with no regard to consequences, as they did. They may think that a whole week of fire-tending by the altos, trebles, etc. is unrealistic.

7. Students may criticize the desire for good feeling at the expense of truth shown by Ralph at the meeting, and the lack of planning and control that leads to heedless action.

8. Points to mention include: Ralph's acceptance of Jack's ironic failure to use the conch right after its role is announced as he declares the needs for lots of rules and implicitly suggests punishment for those who break them and when Jack (and Simon) interrupt Ralph to add description about the mountain; Jack's failure to look beyond his own desire to hunt and kill to see the effect of his statement on the group and that he may be increasing fear when Ralph is trying to quell it; Jack's taking over "leadership" when he sets off with the disorderly group dashing away to make the fire and Ralph's acceptance of it; Ralph's cooperation with Jack's suggestion to use Piggy's specs; Jack's and Ralph's unspoken agreement to keep Piggy from speaking on the mountain (page 43); Jack's agreement with Ralph about the use of the conch after Jack has just said the conch doesn't count on the mountain (page 44).

9. Points to include: references to hunting and killing; slamming the knife into the tree to illustrate killing the pig (page 32); the implication of punishment for rule breakers (page 33); his "fierce" response to Piggy (page 43), and his speech to Piggy in general. Students may recognize some irony in Jack's statement (page 44) "After all, we're not savages," if not now, then as they read farther.

10. Points to include: lack of planning in general, Jack's choice of a site, desire for big fire rather than a useful fire.

11. Most students may think that he was caught in the fire and died.

Strategy 5: References and Allusions, page 26

1. Answers will vary. Students may mention that the seeming lack of inhabitants on the island is one difference; there has been no reference to religion, let alone Christianity, so that doesn't seem to be a theme. In predicting what WILL happen in *Lord of the Flies,* they may note that the situation of isolation due to war and the violence of adults seems important, as do the hints of foreboding in nature and the streak of violence in Jack's character.

2. Students may focus on the Lord of the Flies' speech to Simon (page 164), "Fancy thinking the Beast was something you could hunt and kill! . . . You knew, didn't you? I'm part of you. Close, close, close! I'm the reason why it's no go? Why things are what they are?"

Strategy 6: Plot Conflict, page 28

1. Students may identify Ralph as the protagonist and his desire to get home as the conflict he faces. This is supported by Ralph being the first character introduced, the bulk of the focus being on him, and the final statement about his interior disposition at the end. Some students may point to a larger issue and discuss the struggle of humanity to build a just society or the difficulty, given human nature, in forming community.
2. Students should identify the conflict or conflicts in each chapter.

Writer's Forum 2: Journal, page 29

1. Answers will vary. Entries should show consistent characterization and be recognizable as belonging to the character the student has identified in point of view, tone, language, maturity, etc.

Chapter 3: Huts on the Beach, page 30

1. Students may note the length of Jack's hair and his freckled and peeling back; the disintegration of his shorts; Ralph's exclamation, "Been working for days now. And look!"; the description of the arrival of evening and the changes in nature that accompany it (pages 60-61).
2. Signs of order and organization include Jack's, Ralph's, and Simon's dedication to duty; the division of labor between hunters and builders; the stash of water; the two standing shelters; the continual meetings. Signs of disorder include the tension between Jack and Ralph; the failure of the group to carry out decisions made at meetings; the collapse of the third shelter; the nightmares; Jack's madness; the inadequacy of the fire.
3. Students may note that: the focus of the bulk of the boys is on having fun; it takes Jack a moment to understand the meaning of the word "rescue" (page 56); although Ralph is still concerned about the adequacy of the fire, he is spending his time on shelters, hoping to quell the littluns' fear.
4. Answers will vary. Students may think that Simon is sensitive and needs time to himself to think or commune with nature.
5. Students should note that fear breaks out every night; that Ralph has become concerned enough to turn his attention to shelters; Simon has introduced the idea that some of the boys think that the island is not good, which Ralph acknowledges as an accurate description; Jack admits to understanding the feeling of fear that the littluns have, although he rejects its validity.
6. Answers will vary, but students may note serious character differences and the narrator's comment "They walked along, two continents of experience and feeling, unable to communicate" (page 58). They may feel that this hostility seems to be a central conflict in the plot and they may feel that it is more likely to grow than to resolve.
7. Answers will vary. Students should support their conclusions with evidence.

Strategy 7: Rhetoric, page 31

1. Answers will vary. Possible answers:

"... the forest further down shook as with the passage of an enraged monster. .." (page 26) describing the fall of the great rock

"Like a bomb" (page 26) describing the fall of the great rock

"... a rock almost detached, standing like a fort. . . . " (page 27)

"The coral was scribbled in the sea as though a giant had bent down to reproduce the shape of the island in a flowing chalk line but tired before he finished." (pages 27–28)

"... the platform, with insect-like figures moving near it" (page 28)

2. Answers will vary. Possible answers:

". . . the shattered rocks lifted up their stacks and chimneys" (page 26) describing the rock formations on the mountain

"candle buds" (page 29) describing the buds on the evergreen bush

". . . the beard of flame . . ." (page 43)

"The squirrel leapt on the wings of the wind . . . " (page 45)

"Piggy glanced nervously into hell. . ." (page 46)

Strategy 8: Irony, page 32

1. Answers will vary. Here are some examples of irony that students might note in Chapter 4: Verbal Irony: Ralph's suggestion that they make an airplane, a TV set and a steam engine (page 70); Dramatic Irony: Readers know before Jack does that a ship went by and there was no smoke signal (pages 71–76); the narrator tells the reader what none of the boys know, though Piggy may suspect: that the civilization they had left "was in ruins" (page 67). Situational Irony: Jack's expectation of praise and glory for killing a pig is not fulfilled (page 74–76)

Writer's Forum 3: List of Rules, page 33

1. Answers will vary. In addition to explicitly stated rules, such as those about the conch, students may mention such things as Jack's and Ralph's loosely concerted efforts to keep Piggy from speaking too much at meetings.

TEST 1: Chapters 1–3, page 34

Vocabulary
1. The words are particular to the choir's activity and apparel and these references become obsolete and irrelevant almost immediately.
2. These are the sounds made as Ralph learns to blow the conch for the first time.
3. These words describe Jack's reaction to the vote for leader, which he loses.

Essays
1. Answers will vary. Accept reasonable responses.
2. Answers will vary. Accept reasonable responses.
3. Answers will vary. Accept reasonable responses. Besides the most obvious choices of Ralph, Jack, and Piggy, students may choose Simon or Roger, both of whom are still somewhat mysterious at this point.
4. Answers will vary. Accept reasonable responses.
5. Answers will vary. Accept reasonable responses. Students should site details from the book to support their hypotheses.

Chapter 4: Painted Faces and Long Hair, page 35

1. Possible response: There was too much to do to have a sense of something missing, of a lack or a need. Hope is only necessary if there is something that is wanted, and without feeling need, hope was unnecessary.
2. There are older boys and littluns, and there are the hunters as a distinct group.
3. Possible response: Roger is restrained only by the vestiges of adult culture that the group maintains and if these are lost, his violence will be uncontrollable.
4. It liberated Jack from himself and thus from the societal constraints he felt on his behavior and created a horrible and fascinated compulsion to obedience in the others.
5. Possible response: Without writing, the boys have (without being conscious of it) lost a lot of the order in their lives. The same is true of the loss of a way to mark the time. With a clock, they might make regular schedules and begin giving order to their lives.

6. He prays (or at least utters the name of God), saying "Oh, God, oh God!" (page 73) and swears, saying "bloody" (page 73). Both of these suggest his feeling of total helplessness and frustration.
7. Possible response: Students may note that it's a comparison with civilization and that it may suggest that Ralph is like a wrathful god.
8. Answers will vary. Some students may be uncomfortable with the pleasure and delight in violence and shedding blood (pages 75-76).
9. Possible response: The use of the words "brilliant" and "fierce" suggest that there is more appeal in Jack's world.
10. Answers will vary. Possible response: Simon was extremely sensitive to the passionate feelings of Piggy's terror and Jack's violence and Ralph's rage.
11. Answers may vary. Students may tend to agree with Ralph.
12. Answers will vary. Possible response: Maybe Simon is acutely embarrassed by the pointed treatment of Piggy when he and Ralph also hadn't hunted.
13. Jack considers the fire irrelevant (page 75); he feels at fault, but doesn't take the situation too seriously (page 76); Jack feels that his apology is sufficient to heal the situation and is angered by Ralph's refusal to accept it (pages 78–79); Ralph's silence makes Jack rage (page 79); Jack is enraged by Simon's ability to give up his share of meat and do without: Jack is using the food to gain power and Simon, through his generosity, has escaped the trap of owing Jack allegiance for the meat. (page 80)

Strategy 9: Point of View, page 37

1. Answers will vary. Possible responses:
    "Ralph reached inside himself for the worst word he knew. 'They let the bloody fire go out." (page 73)

    "Unwillingly Ralph felt his lips twitch; he was angry with himself for giving way." (page 78)

    "Ralph's mouth watered. He meant to refuse meat, but his past diet of fruit and nuts, with an odd crab or fish, gave him too little resistance." (page 80)

2. Answers will vary. Possible responses:
    Simon: "Simon lowered his face in shame." (page 80)

    Jack: "He looked in astonishment, no longer at himself, but at an awesome stranger." (page 68)

    Henry: "He became absorbed beyond mere happiness as he felt himself exercising control over living things." (page 66)

    Maurice: "Maurice still felt the unease of wrongdoing." (page 65)

    Piggy: "Daring, indignant, Piggy took the conch." (page 45)

3. He is outside the action, but knows what happens and the characters thoughts and feelings about the action. Students may note that at the same time, there seems to be more sympathy for Ralph, Simon, and Piggy, and less for Jack.

4. Third-person omniscient point of view

Writer's Forum 4: Dialogue, page 38

1. Piggy speaks in a lower-class dialect characterized by:

    can't for *can* "I can't hardly move with all these creeper things" (page 1)

    dropping prepositions "All [of] them other kids" (page 2)

    incorrect verb form "When we was coming down . . . "; "And this is what the cabin done." (page 3)

    incorrect demonstratives "Them fruit" (page 4)

    double negatives "I didn't expect nothing." (page 8)

    He also speaks frequently in admonitions and reproofs.

2. Answers will vary. Each person in the dialogue should have consistent characterization through his or her speech.

Chapter 5: Beast from Water, page 39

1. Students should note that he suddenly sees the lack of personal hygiene, the lack of attention to detail in their construction efforts, the difference between his ability to reason and Piggy's.
2. He remembers the boy with the mulberry birthmark speaking at an assembly. He feels guilty because the boy died in the fire, and even though he wouldn't admit it when it happened, Ralph knows it.
3. Answers will vary. Sometimes addressing fears can make people put them in perspective. Sometimes mentioning fears can spread them.
4. Possible response: He means that everything is understandable and explainable by scientific inquiry except that people, for reasons he does not explain, may not be susceptible to this kind of analysis.
5. Answers will vary. Accept reasonable responses.
6. Possible response: He is trying to explain that all people could have some evil or malformation in them that would make them in some way bestial.
7. They speak "savagely" and used vulgarities such as "sod you" and "nuts." Jack's single syllable was probably a word for excrement.
8. Answers will vary. Accept reasonable responses, supported by evidence from the text. Students may connect Piggy's idea of savagery with his critiques of the group: not following the rules, not planning, hunting (indulging in violence?), irresponsible behavior such as failing to maintain the fire.
9. Jack objects to the fact that Ralph can "sit" and tell people what to do, and he questions: Ralph's qualifications for leadership ("You can't hunt, you can't sing…" page 101); the democratic process itself ("Why should choosing make any difference?"); and the usefulness of Ralph's orders ("orders that don't make any sense"). He accuses Ralph of favoring Piggy, and he decries the need for rules. Students' assessments of the validity of each criticism will vary. Accept reasonable responses.
10. Answers will vary. Accept reasonable responses based on evidence from the text. Students may agree with the hints Simon has given that there is a beast in human nature; or they may think that there is a ghost; or no beast; etc.
11. Possible response: That they are: helpless; at the mercy of powerful forces much greater than they are; lacking direction; etc.
12. Students will likely agree with Piggy's analysis, and should support their conclusions with evidence.
13. Possible response: Since Golding presents adults as even more violent and destructive than children (engaging in a war using atomic weapons), the answer must be no.

Strategy 10: Setting and Mood, page 42

Students should show awareness of the various uses of setting. In the early chapters, they should note the obstacles the setting creates to being rescued. In the last chapters, they should note the obstacles and opportunities that the setting creates for Ralph as he tries to avoid being murdered.

Writer's Forum 5: Persuasive Speech, page 43

1. Students' essays should counter both Jack's and Ralph's arguments against Ralph remaining chief with arguments and information that convincingly show that Ralph's leadership is best for all.

Chapter 6: Beast from Air, page 44

1. The irony stems from a) the fact that in a godless world, Ralph's prayer, "If only they could send us something grownup . . . a sign or something" (page 105) has been answered; and b) the fact that Ralph was looking to the grownup world for wisdom and the sign was a decaying body of a man who died in the war, a sign of the violence and lack of understanding that permeates the adult world. This shows that the boys' confidence in adults expressed at the end of Chapter 5 is completely misplaced, and is an indication that there is no hope in the mere fact of growing up. Ironically, the most hopeful sign seems to be the boys themselves (Ralph, Piggy, and Simon) who are aware that things aren't right. [You may wish to note later that, ironically, the distorted worship of "the beast" that arises from the appearance of this "sign" is partially responsible for the murders of Simon and Piggy and the attempted murder of Ralph.]

3. Answers will vary. Students should note Jack's rejection of democracy, his attempts to shortcut the democratic process of debate, his lack of interest in the "poor" of the island society (the littluns) which seems to indicate a sort of "survival of the fittest" mentality, and his definition of the elite—those who "ought to say things" (page 114).

4. Simon sees humanity as having two natures: heroic and sick (page 116).

5. Students should note Jack's delight in a place that Ralph finds unhealthy and oppressive, and Jack's fascination with violence and destruction.

6. Answers will vary. Accept reasonable responses. Students may possibly feel that Ralph is not up to the burden of being the voice of reason for all his peers and the stress is affecting his ability to think.

7. Answers will vary. Accept reasonable responses. Students may predict that "the beast" will or will not be found; that Jack and Ralph will have another confrontation; that the fire will or will not be relit; that the potential for a group living at the castle may become important.

Strategy 11: Symbolism, page 46

1. Answers will vary. Students may say that Piggy stands for intelligence and respect, Ralph for responsible leadership and democratic community, Simon for prophetic vision, and Jack for elitism, violence, and unbridled passion. Ralph and Jack can be seen broadly as the two aspects of humanity in Simon's vision, vying for control. Intelligence and sensitive vision are killed in the struggle between them. While the "sick" man does not kill the "heroic man," he may have succeeded, by the end, in killing his hope and his spirit.

TEST 2: Chapters 4–6, page 47

Vocabulary

1. These obscenities show the increasing lack of restraint the boys feel about their behavior, their growing incivility to each other, and in particular, lack of respect for Simon and Ralph.

Essay Topics

1. Students should discuss the claims for Ralph; for Ralph, Simon, and Piggy; for the whole little community under Ralph's care, guidance, and leadership. The conflicts they choose will partly depend on the protagonist they identify, but will likely include the conflict between the boys and the beast without, the boys and the beast within, and between Jack and Ralph/the community.

2. Answers will vary. Accept reasonable responses.

3. Answers will vary. It may emerge that students like the two characters in different ways: Ralph has more appealing surface characteristics and Piggy is whiny and annoying, although Piggy, because of his intellect and loyalty, might be the character students would prefer as a sole companion on a deserted island.

4. Answers will vary. Accept reasonable responses.

5. Students should mention personal, religious, and social groups, for example, friends, family, school, church; cultural items, such as clothes, particular foods; places, such as their homes, etc.

6. Students should consider Jack's criticisms as well as the signs of disorder they were asked to write about earlier.

Chapter 7: Shadows and Tall Trees, page 48

1. Students should note the signs of regression in Ralph's behavior (biting his nails); the way his norms have slipped; and his desire for life as he knew it at home, even to the point of wishing for soap and a toothbrush—two things teen-aged boys are supposedly notoriously uninterested in.

2. Answers will vary. Possible response: Simon seems to have interrupted Ralph in order to reassure him, in the face of his growing hopelessness, that he has reason to hope— Ralph will return home. It is presented as a prophetic utterance, although Simon's reticence makes him back off the certainty of his statement. Students' opinions about whether Ralph will get back will vary. Students may interpret Ralph's smile as belief in Simon's statement, or simply as gratitude for Simon's concern and good wishes.

3. Answers will vary. Possible response: It is a way of showing the intimacy and extremity of Jack's involvement in the hunt, and suggests that his violent passion for hunting goes beyond appropriate bounds.

4. People use fantasy to distance themselves from the present, to recapture a past that they love, to encourage their hope in the future, because what they want would be inappropriate to act out in the real world, and less damaging/harmful/inappropriate in a fantasy.

5. Answers will vary. Students should note the seduction of Ralph into what might be called the hunting mentality, the re-enactment that quickly turns into real violence, the excitement that overtakes the group, the ritual chant, the overcoming of all morals and standards by "the desire to squeeze and hurt" which was "overmastering," the concern with status, Robert's suggestion to switch back to reality by using a real pig, and Jack's suggestion that they murder a littlun, which draws laughter(!).

6. The narrator's first sentence in that description makes Ralph sound like a studious and careful thinker with meticulous habits. The following sentence undercuts the first, showing that all the care is for nothing, since Ralph doesn't have the capability to think clearly enough to make all the effort he puts into it worthwhile. Perhaps he would do better to consult Piggy.

7. His sarcasm shows his hatred of Piggy and his resentment of what he seems to consider Ralph's special treatment of Piggy.

8. It's ironic that the boys react to a plain reference to the truth as if it were something indecent.

9. Most students will be surprised. Astute students may pick up the repetition of forms of *dark/darkness* on pages 136–137, and the connection of darkness with Roger, whom the narrator calls "a dark figure," and the sense of impending evil.

10. Students may note the following:

    Roger: is characterized by the narrator as impervious. This and the fact that he irritates Ralph with his tapping, contribute to making him unsympathetic.

    Ralph: That "his voice spoke for him" and he "bound himself together with his will" seems to indicate his courage; told from Ralph's perspective at end.

    Jack: Sarcastic; courageous in going alone and in re-ascending with the other two; "in the rear, for all his brave words"; taunting of Ralph, when he asks him, "scared?"

Answer Pages

Strategy 12: Foreshadowing and Flashback, page 50

1. Answers will vary. Possible response: Eric's recollection of the first fire (page 109). It resonates with Ralph's flashback on page 95, and suggests the far-reaching effects that lack of planning and irresponsible action has on these boys' minds and hearts.

2. Answers will vary. Possible response: The weather through Chapters 8–9 (including the thunder that starts on page 158, and continues on pages 161, 163, 166, 173–175) and the narrator's comment, "Evening was come, not with calm beauty but with the threat of violence" (page 172), coupled with the other descriptions of the weather. This violence in the natural world that hints at the violence that will occur at the hands of human beings is derived both from the setting and from the narrator. Students are likely not to think the weather is a foreshadowing the first time it is mentioned.

Chapter 8: Gift for the Darkness, page 51

1. Students should note that Ralph rarely uses bad language, but he did when the fire went out (Chapter 4, page 73). In both situations, he is facing monumental fears: fear of being stuck on the island forever, and fear of death. He seems to use bad language as an outlet when he is pushed nearly to the breaking point.

2. Students may mention the following: Ralph says "Even Jack 'ud hide" (page 142); Ralph calls the hunters "boys armed with sticks" (page 142); Jack doesn't respect Ralph's leadership qualities— "He's like Piggy. . . . He isn't a proper chief. . . . He's a coward himself" (page 144); Jack doesn't get away with the lies he tells about Ralph (page 144); Ralph doesn't hunt, doesn't hold the position of prefect, and he is not one of Jack's group, known to him from before the island time (page 144); Ralph catches Jack in the contradiction of complaining about talk when Jack insisted that he get credit for calling the meeting and Jack is pretty much the only one talking (page 144); apparently no one votes to remove Ralph from office, and Jack is mortified (pages 144–145).

3. Piggy, who first brings it up at the end of Chapter 5, in the conversation that leads up to his saying, "if you stand out of the way, he'd hurt the next thing" (pages 103–104) and in Chapter 8 when he says, "I expect it's him" in answer to Ralph's question about why things are breaking up (pages 159–160).

4. Possible response: It resonates with his quick recovery from his feelings of guilt when he let the fire go out in Chapter 4 and his attitude toward the fire later: he doesn't seem to treat their situation with the gravity it deserves; he is still a willful child, getting meat for the others because the hunt satisfies his lust and because it gives him power over the others, not out of a sense of responsibility or community.

5. Answers will vary. Possible response: When the narrator describes the silence after Jack calls for a vote as "full of shame" (page 144), it may indicate Jack's shame and humiliation or it may indicate that the boys are too ashamed to indicate their support of Jack publicly (perhaps because somewhere in their hearts they acknowledge that Ralph speaks to more noble sentiments in them), and instead of acknowledging him as their leader in public, they sneak away and make him chief. The reference to the former achievements of the choir—that "their voices had been the song of angels" (page 151) contrasts with the word *demoniac* (page 160), which is what they have become, and points to Simon's insight (page 116) that in human beings dwell both the heroic and the sick; the angelic and the bestial.

6. Students should mention the following: Ralph's first thought is for the viability of the continual smoke signal; after this he reflects his own fear, the irrationality of the other boys' behavior, his own lapses into uncaring, and the roots of the break-up of their society; he comes to openly rely more on Piggy. Piggy feels relief and freedom with Jack's departure, and is able to contribute more to the community, which gratifies him; he introduces the first gesture of pure altruism in the book—the gathering of fruit for Ralph; he risks personal danger and exerts himself physically to save the conch from the savages.

7. Students may mention the following words: *civility, respect, kindness, friendship, civilization.* They may note that Jack uses food to gain power, while Piggy uses it to cement community.

8. Students may see that Piggy seems to have a blind spot concerning Simon, dismissing him as "cracked" without understanding him.

9. Students should convey Simon's encounter with the Lord of the Flies, ending when he looses consciousness in an epileptic seizure. They may understand it as a real and prophetic experience or as Simon's imagination coupled with rational insights.

10. Simon suggests confronting the terrible reality face-to-face. Jack's reaction seems contradictory: first he says that his tribe will "forget the beast," but then—perhaps because he sees the "fervor" of the tribe's reaction to this statement (page 152) and sees in it a new avenue to hold more power over them, he initiates a religion of the beast by making the propitiatory offering of the sow's head.
    Ralph's immediate reaction is defeat. Piggy accepts the limitations of the beast's presence and searches for practical ways to work around them.

11. Students should note the sexual imagery that parallels both a wedding and a rape: the drops of blood as the pig is first violated, and the suggestive phrases "wedded to her in lust," "excited by the long chase," "hurled themselves at her," "dreadful eruption," "squealed and bucked," "found a lodgement for his point and began to push till he was leaning with his whole weight. The spear moved forward inch by inch," "The sow collapsed under them and they were heavy and fulfilled upon her" (page 154).

12. For Jack the head is part of a ritual of propitiation, perhaps the beginnings of a religion of which he is the chief and only priest. To Simon it seems to be something along the lines of the devil: a tempter and tormentor who uses but also twists the truth.

13. The island has not changed—it is the people on the island who are changing. Ralph is trying to convey the disintegration of their island society and the hopelessness he feels, but he is externalizing the problems to nature and the presence of the beast and not seeking the source of the problem in the hearts of people.

14. Ralph is somewhat inarticulate about his fear (page 159), but besides fearing the beast (which he puts in a special category) he seems to fear: the inability of the other boys to comprehend the seriousness of their situation and the importance of the fire in that context; the unreasonableness of not following through on the act that is in your power and which will (in his analogies) undoubtedly lead to your well-being; his own lapses into uncaring; the disintegration of their society.

15. It freed him from shame and self-consciousness.

16. He was trying to save the conch, which is what he thought they'd come to steal.

17. Students should note that: Jack disregards the welfare of the littluns; he rules by edict rather than democratic dialogue; he makes himself high priest, as well as chief, and creates rituals of power around both offices; he acts for immediate gratification rather than planning for the future (e.g. killing the nursing sow, rather than a boar); he encourages (through the hunt and through make-up, nakedness, etc.) the unbridled giving way to passions; he makes decisions in order to gain more power over his followers; his rule is based on savagery, rather than on clinging to what vestiges they can manage of the civilization they left.

18. Possible response: He tempts Simon to betray his integrity in order to achieve status with the other boys, particularly Ralph; he refers to Simon's understanding (page 116) that the beast is interior—part of the human make-up, but he suggests that Simon leave this knowledge behind so that he can rejoin the other boys in camaraderie; when Simon apparently refuses, he threatens Simon with death and names the murderers.

Chapter 9: A View to a Death, page 54

1. Students should include the following details: Jack appears like an idol (page 170); normality is found in abuse of Piggy (page 171); power is based on control of the food source (page 172); a ritual dance that builds to a frenzy and loss of individual will and inhuman murder (page 174).

2. Possible response: The narrator is presenting the point of view of the boys. Students may mention that Simon was also identified with the beast on pages 93–94 of Chapter 5. Students may feel disgust at the abandonment of humanity that the dancers/murderers undergo.

3. Possible responses: the refusal of humanity throughout its history to listen to the prophetic voices that arise; the fate of the individual standing alone against the collective; the suffering of the sensitive individual in an insensitive world.

4. Simon is coming to free them from "the beast," and they understand him to BE the beast. Simon is the only one who knows what the real beast is. He is the most gentle and harmless of all the boys. The Lord of the Flies told him in the vision that "Jack and Roger and Maurice and Robert and Bill and Piggy and Ralph" would kill him.

5. Possible response: they may use the same responses as when the boy with the birthmark died: denial, evasion, trying to forget.

Strategy 13: Names and Euphemisms, page 56

1. Possible response: Jack supplants Ralph as chief for most of the boys on the island. One of Ralph's chief qualities is his unselfish attempts to get them all rescued. Simon's attentiveness and sensitivity are part of his prophetic role.

2. Answers will vary. Students may see a connection between Roger's lust for violence and the connection of his name with a weapon.

3. Students should note the lust for killing pigs, the killing of the sow as a turning point in the plot because it makes clear that the boys' hunt is a perversion of the orderly foray to get food, and the killing of Piggy as an extension of that perverted desire to impose suffering on the weak, and meaningless and indefensible destruction of life. The connection between pigs and Piggy is explicitly drawn in Chapter 5, pages 91–92: "What would a beast eat?" "Pig." "We eat pig." "Piggy!"

4. Answers will vary. Possible response: The namelessness of adults is appropriate since for all intents and purposes they are out of the picture, irrelevant to what happens (other than their role in causing the violence that gave rise to the situation). The namelessness of the young children might symbolize the loss of the next generation, and the failure of the elders to take responsibility for and nurture those who follow, which is the only way to perpetuate a society. Students should also note that in Chapter 12 almost all of the boys have lost their names and their individual identities: they are "the savage," simply a member of the tribe, absorbed into the collective. The lack of names for plants and animals might point to the dislocation the boys feel or their lack of interest in identifying the natural phenomena in their surroundings, which might symbolize their inability or refusal to grasp the real possibility that they might be stranded forever and need to know more about their surroundings.

5. Possible response: There is no reason, in this situation at least, to distinguish the two personalities, since they act, think, and speak as one.

Writer's Forum 6: Compare and Contrast Essay, page 57

1. Answers will vary. Possible response: responsibility for others (particularly the young); meeting basic needs; planning for the future; knowledge; decision-making process; dignity/civility; rationality.

2. Students should touch on the following: socioeconomic status; social status; role in island society; character strengths and weaknesses; altruism; foresight.

Writer's Forum 7: Poetry—An Elegy for Simon, page 58

1. Poems will vary. If the poem is written from a particular character's point of view, the diction, tone, and thoughts should fit that character. The style of the poem should be consistent and meaningfully related to the content.

TEST 3: Chapters 7–9, page 59

Vocabulary

1. It describes the various reactions of Jack, Roger, and Ralph as they go up the mountain to face the beast.

Essay Topics

1. Possible response: any external fear—though it may be terrible, haunting, and the result of violence—is explicable and not supernaturally terrifying. It is the darkness and evil inside the hearts of people, the beast within, that we must struggle to come to terms with.
2. Students should mention Piggy's lower-class dialect and his reasoning-out-loud, Samneric's joint monologues. Those who engage in dialogue without interruptions show the most respect for the democratic process of decision-making.
3. Possible responses: order, democracy, respect, debate, civilization.
4. Students should touch on the following: the lust for violence; the desire for meat; the ritual that began with the beating of Robert (page 129), fear of the beast and the storm, desire for a scapegoat, mob mentality.
5. Students should touch on: the disregard for the future shown in killing a mother, thus orphaning her babies and reducing the future food supply; they may mention the wanton violence of thrusting the spear into the sow's anus and the sexual innuendos implicit in the description (including the boys' reactions to the killing); the laughter following the sow's death; the decapitating of the sow and the inauguration of the cult of the beast with the creation of the Lord of the Flies. They may see this incident as a sign of the growing decadence of the society that is turning more and more towards evil.
6. Students may note: the association of the beast with the dark, including the statement by one of the boys that the beast comes "out of the dark," and the use of the words *dark/darkness* on pages 136–137 in relation to Roger and the climb up the mountain to search for the beast; the loss of brightness in Simon's eyes as he went up the mountain to confront the beast (page 167); the importance of fire and light in the story; etc.

Chapter 10: The Shell and the Glass, page 60

1. Possibly both terms are symbolic: Piggy's sight must have been impaired to allow him to take part in the murder of Simon; their bodies are befouled, not only by the accumulated grime of their island stay, but by participating in the murder.
2. At first, Ralph is honest. He calls Simon's death "murder," even when Piggy tries to shut him up, and ameliorate the situation, suggesting that maybe Simon isn't really dead, and to get out of responsibility for Simon's death. Ralph sees that it is themselves they have to fear. Eventually, they both decide to lie, so that when they meet Sam and Eric, who also lie, the narrator tells us that "memory of the dance that none of them had attended shook all four boys convulsively" (page 182).
3. Possible response: while his followers both hope and believe that the beast is now dead, Jack uses their fears and their trust in his greater understanding of how the beast operates to enhance his power over the others by claiming that the beast is not dead and making plans to propitiate it.
4. Here it is used as a matter of course to describe any individual member of Jack's tribe. It is a sign of the regression of the society.
5. It is in some ways reminiscent of the killing of the sow, in that there is a sadistic pleasure taken in the infliction of pain, but whereas that had the purpose of procuring

food, Wilfrid has not committed any identifiable transgression, and the punishment, along with the waiting period, seem completely gratuitous.

6. Ralph says (page 187), "We might get taken prisoner by the Reds." Students may connect the book to Cold War fears about Communism.

7. Answers will vary. Accept reasonable responses supported by evidence from the text. Students may suggest that he is having a kind of seizure.

8. Students may note that although Ralph said, "Oh, God, oh God" when he saw the ship and realized the fire was out (page 73), this is the first text identified explicitly as a prayer, and it is a horrible, self-centered, cruel request.

9. Ralph fought someone whose fingers he bit and who hit him in the face. Ralph got on top and smashed the person repeatedly in the mouth. He was then kneed in the groin. Eric's description of being smashed in the mouth and kneeing his opponent in the groin can lead to the conclusion that all of Ralph's and Eric's energy was expended on fighting each other. When Ralph "moved suddenly in the dark," (page 194) it may be because he realizes with whom he was fighting.

10. Answers will vary. Students should tell what led them to the realization. Students may have realized, even before this chapter, that control of Piggy's specs, and therefore of fire, was going to become an important issue.

11. Fire is one of the most basic needs—for warmth, and cooking food, and controlling fear in the dark. Without access to fire, Jack's leadership was not complete.

12. Face paint removes self-consciousness and shame (page 160); hides emotions (page 185); and makes individuals into group members first.

Chapter 11: Castle Rock, page 62

1. Possible response: It seems to be a rhetorical question, the answer to which is supposed to be "no," but because the answer has been called into question (particularly by the narrator referring to Jack's followers as "savages"), Ralph's whole speech becomes ironic.

2. He is referring to Simon's death. Students may argue that although Jack was the moving force and bears the most responsibility, they all are guilty of Simon's death.

3. Answers will vary. Students should realize that to withhold fire might in some circumstances be equivalent to murder.

4. The statement can be understood in at least three ways. One is that without the fire, it is impossible to believe that anyone will find them, and the odds are they will all die on the island. A figurative interpretation might say that because of the beast in the human heart we can never be rescued or because of the evil these individual young men have committed, they can never be rescued from their guilt.

5. He stops trying to evade the truth, naming Simon's murder for what it was, recognizing his own weaknesses and Jack's strengths, and, as a result, willing to face his enemy without fear for the sake of what's right.

6. Most students will interpret this as the conch, but some may believe it is unflinching honesty. Those who focus on the conch may point out that Jack never does take possession of it.

7. Students should mention the narrator's comment, "They understood only too well the liberation into savagery that the concealing paint brought" (page 199).

8. The infrequent boat traffic and the amount of destruction that seems to have taken place in the world, has made it appear highly unlikely that they will be found without a signal.

9. Possible response: It may seem to them as if unity and support are more important at this moment than strict truth. It seems that Samneric realize that something is missing with Ralph, and they are probably questioning his leadership.

10. Students may mention the following: Piggy's statement, "We may stay here till we die" (page 10); the whole connection between Piggy and the pigs that meet violent ends, particularly on pages 91–92, where the conversation suggests that the beast might eat

Piggy—one could consider Piggy's death as figuratively fulfilling this. That Roger will turn to violence is foreshadowed by the statement, "Some source of power began to pulse in Roger's body" (page 203), and the dropping of stones by Roger with his hand on the lever (page 208).

11. He is appealing to a sense of fairness and shared principles that do not exist.

12. Possible response: Their capture is a violation of two of the most basic rights—to choose with whom to ally oneself and to have free use of one's own body.

13. Answers will vary. Accept reasonable responses supported by the text. Possible responses: Roger's emotion as he kills Piggy; the word *stuff* to describe Piggy's brains; the comparison of Piggy to a pig by the narrator as he twitches after death; the quick disappearance of someone who was so important to the story.

14. Most immediately it was the unwarranted beating of Wilfrid—this led to Roger's reverie on "the possibilities of irresponsible authority," and after this, he quickly unleashes the violence within him that earlier had been kept in check by adult authority, and by its vestiges on the island.

15. Jack meant to kill Ralph with that spear throw.

Strategy 14: Characterization Continuum, page 64

1. Answers will vary. Possible responses may include the following details:

   Self-concerned/community-minded There may be some aspect of community-mindedness in Jack's determination to provide the group with meat, but then again, there may not. Jack is self-concerned throughout, but his self-concern is revealed as growing greater when he rejects Ralph's government and sets himself us as chief, abusing the power he has and using force to gain cooperation. Samneric reach a high point of community-mindedness when they risk harm to help Ralph, after they have been tortured into agreeing to join Jack's tribe of savages. They end up betraying Ralph's hiding place in order to save themselves from more pain after being tortured again.

   Clear thinking/confused Ralph's ability to reason is called into question in his first conversations with Piggy, who points out logical errors in Ralph's wishful or unclear thinking. Ralph achieves more clarity for a while, but as the book goes on, Ralph's clear-headedness, even about the subjects that are of the most importance to him—the smoke and going home—clouds, and he loses the trust of his last followers because of this.

   Kind/cruel Jack is never kind: his rhetoric is dominated by sarcasm at the beginning and threats at the end. As the restraints of the island society weaken, the cruelty and violence of his character gain more expression. Ralph's first appearance shows him to have what might be characterized as "thoughtless cruelty"—careless of Piggy's feelings, not from malice, but from lack of sensitivity and attention. His last thoughts about Piggy, however, show a well from which kindness might, with the proper nurturing, spring. Students may mention one of the few acts of unadulterated kindness in the book, such as Simon getting fruit beyond the reach of the littluns for them, or Piggy and Samneric getting fruit for Ralph.

2. Answers will vary depending on the character chosen.

Writer's Forum 8: A Possible Ending, page 65

1. Answers will vary. Students' endings should provide a conclusion for: whether Samneric join the tribe; what happens to Ralph without Piggy to guide and support him; how the growing violence culminates or is stopped; whether or not the boys get home and how.

Chapter 12: Cry of the Hunters, page 66

1. Answers will vary. Students' responses will depend on what effects they expect adult society to have on the boys. They might expect Jack to be a cult leader and Roger to be a murderer and Ralph to be a government leader.
2. Answers will vary. Students should note the narrator's description of Jack as "a little boy" and offer some ideas about this.
3. Answers will vary. Students should support their answers with quotations from the text.
4. Answers will vary. Many students will have expected Ralph to be caught and killed.
5. Students should mention the main themes of the book in their discussion of change including at least some of the topics listed in the History of Ideas and the Themes on pages 79–89.
6. Students should reflect the boys' hopes and expectations as detailed in Chapter 1, referring to the works of literature that shaped the boys' thoughts, and Ralph's comments on it being a "good island"; Ralph's question to Piggy about things falling apart and his statement that the island was getting worse; the progression from accidental death to murder by a frenzied mob, to the deliberate attempts by Roger to kill Piggy and by Jack and the others to kill Ralph; the change from democracy to a combination of dictatorship and mob rule.
7. Students' answers to this question will depend on how they characterize Golding's view. Some students may focus on the mayhem and the destructive and sick beast each person carries inside. Some may focus on the small acts of kindness, friendship, honesty, and responsibility that still go on despite the grave sickness of humanity. Some may discuss the combination of the "heroic and sick" (page 116). Accept reasonable responses supported by evidence.
8. Answers will vary. Accept reasonable responses supported by evidence.
9. Students may identify as the protagonist: Ralph; the group of Ralph, Piggy, and Simon (possibly including Samneric); or, if they understand this as a fable or parable, people trying to live ethically in a world filled with evil. The antagonist will depend on who they identify as protagonist, possibly: Jack; Jack and Roger; people who lust for power and violence and live unethically. Accept reasonable responses supported by evidence.
10. Answers will vary. Accept reasonable responses supported by evidence.
11. Students should mention the passages that tell of people confronting the beast on the mountain (Jack, Ralph, and Roger; Simon); the description of the fear on the beach that led to Simon's death; and descriptions of Ralph's fear in Chapter 12, particularly: when he imagines Piggy coming out of the water with an empty head (page 221); and Ralph's final run to the beach (pages 231–232).
12. Answers will vary. Accept reasonable responses supported by evidence.
13. Students may include: that the fire set to destroy Ralph was destroying the fruit and would have led to the deaths of all the boys from starvation, had they not been rescued; that the officer thinks at first that they are just playing a game; that the officer, despite being engaged in a war himself, expects children to live together in harmony as in *Coral Island*; that it is only after Piggy's death that Ralph can give him his due and name him as "friend," etc.

Writer's Forum 9: A News Article, page 68

1. Students might choose for an audience the communities in which the boys live, the world, the school that the choir attends, etc. The first paragraph should succinctly sum up the main information about the rescue, cast in a light that fits the audience—that is, keeping in or leaving out information as appropriate. Details should be presented in a reasonable order, and made-up facts should be consistent with the characters and situation. Made-up interviews should have characters speaking from an appropriate point of view, and capitalization and punctuation for quotations should be accurate.

Strategy 15: Consulting Outside References, page 69

No exercise.

Strategy 16: Rereading a Book, page 70

1. Students' second reading should in general be smoother and easier than the first since they have already dealt with the conceptually and emotionally difficult material. What is lacking in suspense the second time through may be compensated by their ability to take in more of the detail and appreciate more of the artistry used in constructing the text.

Strategy 17: Theme, page 72

1. Answers will vary. Students will likely focus on topics mentioned in the History of Ideas and Theme Pages, such as human nature, civilization and culture, government, violence and war, friendship and loyalty, people and nature, leadership and authority, maturity and adulthood, status and reputation, memory and forgetting, reality and responsibility, fear, and the topic of this thematic grouping of literary works: community.

Strategy 18: Comparing and Contrasting a Book and a Movie, page 73

1. Students should address the questions given for guidance. Facts and opinions should be clearly stated and opinions should be supported by evidence. To extend this exercise, have students develop criteria for comparing and contrasting a book and an audio recording, and then compare the book with Listening Library's unabridged version of *Lord of the Flies* read by William Golding.

TEST 4: Chapters 10–12, page 74

Vocabulary

1. the techniques used in hunting Ralph
2. the uniform of the officer whose arrival signals the rescue of the boys from the island

Essay Topics

1. Answers will vary depending on the story chosen. Students might use one of the following: *Robinson Crusoe, The Swiss Family Robinson,* "The Most Dangerous Game," *The Coral Island, Swallows and Amazons, Treasure Island,* etc.
2. Answers will vary depending on the story chosen. Students might use one of the following: *To Kill a Mockingbird, The Unvanquished, The Portrait of the Artist as a Young Man,* "Araby," *The Way of All Flesh, The Giver,* etc.
3. Students should draw parallels between the violence in the world of adults and the violence in the world of the children. In terms of the hunt for Ralph that the officer interrupts, you may want to share with students what Golding says of the ending of the book: "The officer, having interrupted a man-hunt, prepares to take the children off the island in a cruiser which will presently be hunting its enemy in the same implacable way. And who will rescue the adult and his cruiser?" in order to call attention to the parallels between the two man-hunts.
4. Answers will vary. Students should support their opinions with evidence from the book.
5. Illustrations will vary, as will explanations. Both should reflect the text.
6. While there are some suggestions of time passing in the boys' conversation, the students will need to rely on guesswork as well as indications in the text. Accept reasonable responses.
7. Students should note that it shows the impotence of adults in taking responsibility for children and nurturing them, caring for them, and bringing them up. It stresses the impersonality with which adults treat children and emphasizes how little hope for

change there is. Students may feel that ending with Ralph's thought would have created a more positive ending, because his sorrow and insight are among the most hopeful signs in the book of a possibility for a future for humanity.

8. Students should note that the littluns and Piggy are also missing names. Possible response: Omitting names shows the narrowness of the island culture, the lack of concern for things beyond immediate need, the lack of care the older boys show for the littluns, etc. See Strategy page 13 for more details.

9. Answers will vary. Students' opinions of the ending will vary, as will their evaluations of the artistry. Opinions should be supported with details from the book.

10. Answers will vary. The future presented should be consistent with the basic premises of the book including the state of the world and characterization, among other things.

11. Students should recognize in Simon an example of the prophet who is not accepted in the community from which he comes. Simon's main role should be recognized, not as forecasting the future, but as a messenger of insight into the realities of things and the need for change.

History of Ideas, page 75

Human Nature, page 75

1. Students should cite details from the book that show that human nature, even in the young child, is already corrupt and that this corruption may be inevitable, and they may reference Henry throwing sand at Percy and the words of the Lord of the Flies to Simon. They should, however, address the case of Simon, who is not only ethical, but dies trying to save the others from their supernatural fear of a natural object—the dead paratrooper. They may argue that good may spring up, but corruption will destroy what is good. Students may say that it is not clear what the boys would have been like with a better upbringing—for all we know, they might have remained innocent.

2. Students might find hope in Simon's goodness, in Piggy's perseverance, and in Ralph's distress. Simon, faced with the knowledge that evil is inevitable and buried deep within us goes to face the beast on the mountain, and hurries off to tell the others of his discovery in order to spare them any more fear. This argues a deep-seated goodness that counterbalances, counteracts, or at least contends with the evil. Piggy, the object of ridicule and scorn, faces the fact that he is blind and handicapped, and has the courage to keep walking, to do what is right against all odds. Ralph, who has only just escaped a horrible death, looks upon the corruption and weeps, not with relief at his own safety but with compassion for Piggy who died. Other students may suggest that Golding is saying that the best that is in us (as represented by Simon, Piggy, and Ralph) is relatively powerless against the evil destructiveness of our inner selves.

Civilization and Culture, pages 75–76

3. Elements of culture missing on the island might include the following: system of education, etiquette, no property (except the conch and Piggy's glasses), a system of justice, writing, art, music. There is an attempt to use division of labor, but it fails; the societal taboo against murder fails, also. There does evolve a primitive religion—a kind of worship of the beast, with a ritual dance and sacrifice; and a tribal government based on power.

4. Possible response: There is enculturation going on in Jack's tribe as the "religion of the beast" is created and the reign of terror and unbridled violence develops.

5. Possible response: The society (such as it was) on the island seemed to lead the boys towards indulgence in "a reign of the passions" rather than away from it. In Golding's view, however, the corruption does not seem to be in society per se, but in the nature of people.

6. Answers may vary based on criteria, but students are likely to find that the society is savage and cite the worship of the beast, the unjust system of reward and punishment, the introduction of murder on the island, the disregard for responsibility, order, and justice.

Government, pages 76–77

7. Possible response: It could be argued that at the first meeting we see the incipient workings of a democracy, which quickly degenerates into a lawless chaos (people talking, but not acting, promises made but not kept, lack of purpose and focus, inability to keep the fire going, to build useful shelters, etc.). That Jack's rule at the end is a tyranny is easily supported.

8. Possible response: It could point to the fact that in the choosing of both leaders, charisma disguised or outweighed inadequacies in practical matters and in vision. These inadequacies led to failures (Ralph's failure to accomplish the maintenance of the fire, building of shelters, and steady supply of water that were his goal; and Jack's choice to lead his followers to what would have likely been their deaths had they not been rescued, since the fire they set destroyed their food supply).

9. Answers will vary. Possible responses: Piggy: Secretary of State or Vice President; Roger: head of the secret police.

Violence/War, page 77

10. Answers will vary. Possible responses: 1) Since the revelation of Jack's violent nature begins with the sighting of the first pig in Chapter One and since Jack is the paramount hunter, the use of meat for food is always coupled in this book with an unhealthy attitude that relishes inflicting pain and drawing blood. Since Jack's attitude is extreme, it cannot be concluded that Golding is opposed to killing animals for food in general. 2) The contrast Golding creates between the attitudes in gathering fruit for food and killing an animal from the very first sighting of a pig may indicate an awareness of the violent tendencies that killing of any kind introduces or cultivates in humans. If so, Golding may be trying to convey an opposition to the use of animals for food, not for health reasons, but to avoid the violent emotions that killing them triggers in us.

11. Possible response: Golding shows violence seeping down from the top in two ways. First, the violence in the world of adults—the war that leads to the boys' predicament—can be identified as a chief cause in the boys' choice of violence. Even Ralph, who is fairly peaceful at heart, pretends to be a fighter plane, "machine-gunning" Piggy at the very beginning of the book (page 6), and the three boys indulge in gratuitous violence as they explore the island (page 26) when they heave a rock that falls, as one of them says, "Like a bomb!" At a second level, the violence and blood-lust of Jack and his hunters permeates the consciousness and lives of the other boys, at first in the "game" in which Robert pretends to be the pig, and all the boys participating, including Ralph, lose their way in the desire to inflict pain and torment (Chapter 7: pages 129–130). It is also Jack's violence that unleashes Roger's sadism (Chapter 10: pages 183–184) and the violence of the younger boys, as well, as they chase Ralph through the forest in order to kill him and behead him as an offering to the beast. Students' answers about their own beliefs will vary. Students may note that Golding seems to indicate that violence begets violence; that violent adults beget violent children; and that this cycle, unless broken, will allow violence to continue perpetuating itself.

12. Students who consider any kind of violence inhumane may postulate that civilization and warfare are entirely incompatible and that warfare is never justified. At the other

end of the spectrum, there may be students who think that war is justified or necessary for a variety of reasons, ranging from the view that only self-defense justifies war to the outlook that war is a valid technique for achieving less pristine political ends.

Themes, page 78

Friendship and Loyalty, page 78

1. Answers will vary. Students may have concepts that include complete honesty, mutual interests, commitment, common beliefs and/or attitudes, respect. They may distinguish friendship from partnerships such as lab partners, business partners, spouses, neighbors, co-workers, siblings, any of which may be friends, but aren't necessarily.

2. Possible response: "Loyalty and disloyalty" is a fundamental theme in the book. Loyalty is what keeps Ralph true to his goals, and what keeps Piggy true to Ralph, despite good reasons to abandon him. Disloyalty is what make boys agree to something at a meeting but fail to carry it out, and what leads Jack, and others, to defect from Ralph's group.

3. Answers will vary, depending on students' definitions of friendship. Some students may even feel that Ralph doesn't make a very good friend to Piggy until the end. Some may feel that the closeness of Samneric doesn't qualify as friendship because it seems so inevitable—that they are not distinguished enough that their relationship fits the kind of relationships we consider to be friendships. Most students will feel that the unspoken understandings and common beliefs held by Roger and Jack do not qualify as friendship, although they may be hard-pressed to explain why they feel as they do, since the relationship has a lot of qualities that are often considered valuable parts of a friendship.

4. Possible response: At first, the narrator calls Jack, Ralph, and Simon friends (page 28), but since their relationship is based on fallacious ideas about the island (that they have the right to dominate it and that it will prove an Edenic paradise) and cruel exclusion of Piggy from the group, it is hard to tell what this friendship means. Since Piggy is the only person identified as a friend at the end of the book (page 235), Golding's attitude toward friendship can most likely be seen in the way Piggy lives his friendship with Ralph. Students may note that he is loyal to Ralph's goals, ignores Ralph's faults, tries to make up for Ralph's failings, supplies help in areas that he sees are Ralph's weaknesses and his strengths, supports Ralph when he's discouraged, etc. Students may think that Golding would identify neither Samneric nor Roger and Jack as friends.

5. Answers will vary. Students may develop the idea that in a world without salvation, friendship is the best hope for humankind to find a way through the darkness brought on by our troubled natures.

People and Nature, page 79

1. Students may say that it appears benevolent and malevolent by turn, and agree with Emerson's characterization.

2. Students may point out that sometimes events in nature seem to foreshadow the violence of humans (the "skull-like coconuts" page 5); sometimes nature seems to be an antagonist (the storm in which the "blows of the thunder were only just bearable," page 174); sometimes a helper (fresh water, the fruit, and the pigs for food). Sometimes people can master nature (by violence, when they burn the forest). Sometimes, though, nature may overmaster humans (the parachutist, nodding even though dead). Students may conclude that in short, nature seems arbitrary: its assistance or imposition is a matter of interpretation and situation.

3. Students should recognize that the boys initially identify the island as an Edenic place ("it's a good island" page 34) to which they come to take charge by right (" This belongs to us," page 27; "savored the right of domination" page 28).

4. Students should refer to the **impediments** caused by ground cover etc.; **assistance** provided by natural sources of food, the bathing pool, etc.; **foreshadowing** indicated by descriptions of natural phenomena (the "skull-shaped coconuts" page 5; "Evening was come, not with calm beauty but with the threat of violence" page 172 on the night Simon is murdered; etc.); **revelation of personality** revealed in Ralph's and (especially) Jack's choice of a site of operations.

5. Students should note that Golding describes the mark of the plane cabin as a "scar;" that on their first day they start a fire that burns out of control and destroys a lot of vegetation (as well as killing at least one child); that after a while, they get lazy and start defecating wherever they happen to be; and that the boys end by starting a fire that burns most of the island, including the fruit, and likely, the pigs. The stay of the boys has proved very destructive to the island from start to finish.

6. Answers will vary. Possible response: Students may point out that anthropologists might think that the people on the island were uncivilized adults engaged in inter-tribal warfare.

Leadership and Authority, page 80

1. Answers will vary. Students should recognize that governments are invested with (or seize) authority and that authority should be (but isn't always) allocated to those of excellent character in order that they may carry out their trust with integrity.

2. Possible responses include: The boys pay heed to Ralph (honest leadership), Jack (charismatic machismo), Roger (unbridled evil), the Beast (fear, chaos, evil), Piggy (scientific thought, logic, and reason).

3. Students may think that Piggy's wisdom and Ralph's practical good sense deserved respect, but that charisma, and fear had the greatest power. Students may recognize that Simon had authority (he was right that Ralph would go home; he understood the true nature of the beast—the beast that dwells within the human heart and leads it to evil; he sensed that going up the mountain was the way to dispel the power of the "external" Beast), but it went unheeded, and was destroyed.

4. Students should mention that Ralph received power by election, Piggy by the appeal of good advice and loyalty, Jack by the attraction of his charisma and the promise of meat, Roger through fear of torture, the Beast through the tortured imaginations of corrupt humanity.

5. Students may judge that Ralph essentially loses his power; that Jack keeps his because of Roger's presence and the fear Roger inspires; that the Beast keeps power because it serves Jack's purposes so he doesn't allow it to be dispelled (page 185); that Piggy keeps power because he is wise and true; that Roger keeps power because he will destroy anyone who doesn't accept him.

6. Students may refer to Ralph's personal failings; to the lack of enforcement. They may suggest that it is impossible that he could have provided the kind of leadership that would have been necessary to govern the boys well, considering their ages and lack of internal discipline.

7. Answers will vary. Accept reasonable responses. Students may choose not to make anything white.

8. Answers will vary. Students may conclude that Golding is suggesting that power and authority naturally fall into the hands of those who are ill-equipped to exercise it justly, but are well able to keep it. They may think that a joint government formed by Piggy, Simon, and Ralph would have been the most effective and fairest.

9. Answers will vary. Students may point to the mutual guilt that began with the death of the boy with the birthmark after Jack exuberantly led the group to start making a fire without forethought, and continued with the violent and unnecessary death of the mother pig, with the outrageous attack on Robert, with the murders of Simon and Piggy, and with the complicity and fear that resulted from all of these as being the main factors contributing to Jack's power.

10. Answers will vary. Students may say that Ralph's increasing loss of control and increasing acceptance of the state on the island as "normal" meant that his administration was doomed. They may conclude that there was nothing else for Piggy to do in any case, or that if they had been Piggy, they would have ceased supporting Ralph in order to do something else. Or, students may say that not only did Piggy's loyalty give Ralph's administration its only hope, but that he had a moral obligation, both for the sake of friendship and particularly for the littluns, to bolster Ralph's administration and give Ralph a chance against Jack, and that it would have been wrong for Piggy to cease his support.

Maturity and Adulthood, page 81

1. Answers will vary. Some students may take the change as purely one of age and physical development. Others may suggest that other qualities are necessary.

2. Answers will vary. Students may refer to maturity; physical, emotional, and psychological development; knowledge; wisdom; privileges based on age (voting, etc.); responsibilities in family and society.

3. Answers will vary. Some students may feel that maturity is a result, not only of having attained a certain age, but of experience, attitudes such as responsibility and commitment, and other virtues. They may point to people who are not yet adults, but show maturity, and adults who do not exhibit the same qualities.

4. Answers will vary. Students should refer to a democracy's need to educate voters—literate, discerning, attentive adults who will carry out their full function as citizens. They may think that people without well-formed characters will not make good, law-abiding citizens. Society also has certain requirements—it needs workers, including leaders and law makers, and people capable of making and keeping the commitments of marriage including raising children. It is also necessary to pass on our culture. Students may also say that education is to make us civilized and to help us stay civilized under trying conditions. Students' evaluation of the relationship between education and adulthood and maturity will depend on their definitions of adulthood and maturity and whether education, in their experience, encourages growth towards these goals.

5. Answers will vary. Students may note that besides the references to the choir, the lack of references to school, on the whole, indicate the uselessness of what was taught there in the boys' present situation. It doesn't seem that the boys' schooling has helped most of them to maintain their virtue in this difficult situation or to plan effective ways of living and working together.

6. Answers will vary. Students may discuss character education, life skills, and child development as courses of study that might have improved the situation.

7. Answers will vary. Students should cite some of the situations in which Piggy uses the expression: notably, the first time, when the boys, led by Jack, rush off and build the destructive fire that causes the first death (pages 38 and 47) and when he addresses Jack just before his death (page 208). Piggy, more than the others, is able to maintain an idea of maturity from the "other world," while trying to keep its values on the island. Students may agree that Piggy's criticisms are just, if not calculated to be rhetorically persuasive.

8. Answers will vary somewhat. Possible responses: Ralph, we are told directly (page 235) learns "the darkness of man's heart" and the value of Piggy, which is invisible to the eye. Piggy learns courage and is able to face both the truth—going from denying that Simon was murdered (page 180) and twisting facts to cover up his involvement to accepting the brutal facts of reality (page 197)—and his physical fears, standing up to Jack (page 208). Simon learns what the Beast truly is, and that he will die (pages 164–165). Jack learns how to gain power.

9. Answers will vary. Accept reasonable responses.

Answer Pages

Status and Reputation, page 82

1. Answers will vary. Accept reasonable responses.
2. Answers will vary. Accept reasonable responses.
3. Students should refer to the governments of Ralph and Jack and the change from Ralph's to Jack's; to the special role of the choir boys; to the distinction between the older boys and the littluns; to the scapegoat roles of Simon and Piggy. Ideas about the most influential factor in forming the hierarchies will vary. Suggestions might include charisma, machismo, violence, lack of morality, and guilt. Some students may realize that racism and sexism have been excluded from the discussion by the fact that it seems that all the characters are white males.
4. Students should refer to the quotation ". . . there was a stillness about Ralph as he sat that marked him out: there was his size, and attractive appearance; and most obscurely, yet most powerfully, there was the conch. The being that had blown that, had sat waiting for them on the platform with the delicate thing balanced on his knees, was set apart." (pages 19–20). Answers as to why Ralph lost status will vary. Possible responses include that: no one could maintain status for long in that group because they were too young and immature to have a fully functioning society; Ralph's inadequacies were revealed with time; Jack's leadership qualities became more appealing; the boys focused less on rescue and the future and more on immediate needs as time went on: meat for dinner was more appealing than keeping up a fire that might have no use; Ralph lost some of the qualities that made him appealing—his standards for personal appearance changed (page 124), and he began to have periods of memory loss and to prefer daydreaming to reality. Jack had leadership qualities and was a "gung-ho" type of person. His exuberance and determination were appealing. Answers to the question about Jack's change in status will vary. Students should note that Jack has a fall in status (recall the election he calls in which he loses ignominiously, pages 144–145. Possible responses include those mentioned for Ralph, as well as the appeal of violence (for example, to Roger); and the persuasiveness of Roger's presence in Jack's group.
5. Most students will say no, citing Piggy's physical disabilities and lack of charisma as making him, in most people's minds, ineligible for leadership roles. Answers about Roger and Jack will vary, since Roger only rose to power at the very end. Some students may believe that if Roger had challenged Jack, he might have ended up killing his opponent and taking over.
6. Piggy ("Piggy was a bore; his fat, his ass-mar and his matter-of-fact ideas were dull, but there was always a little pleasure to be got out of pulling his leg, even if one did it by accident," thinks Ralph, page 70), Simon ("He's cracked," says Piggy, page 151), and Jack (". . .what makes break up like they do?" ". . . I expect it's him." "Jack?" "Jack." pages 159–160) are talked about behind their backs. Accept reasonable responses.
7. Piggy and Simon seem to have the greatest gap between their true character and public estimation.
8. Based on the migration of the community to support Jack, and Roger's murder of Piggy, it appears that Roger exerted far more influence. Both the community and Ralph found that it was possible to discount Piggy, but not Roger. Students may account for this by suggesting that, to a person in danger, terror is far more persuasive than reason.
9. Possible responses include that Simon didn't have charisma; that his understandings were not what the community wanted to hear; that Simon's reputation was based on non-essential points (that he fainted) and misunderstandings (Ralph thinking him gay and wicked, page 59), and he was not really known by the others.

Memory and Forgetting, page 83

1. Answers will vary. Students may say that personal memories ground us, give us identity, help us establish values, teach us, help us relate ourselves to the world—

finding similarities and differences between and among ourselves and others, etc. Facts help us understand the world around us and from that we can determine how to relate to the world; knowledge can help us avoid past errors. Historical and cultural memories are important to society because they pass on society's values and understandings.

2. Answers will vary. Students' opinions about remembering and forgetting may be highly personalized. Some may say that memories are an essential part of who we are and need to be cherished, even if they're painful. Some may say that certain memories can trap us and only forgetting can free us. Students may say that we forget the painful, the trivial (either objectively trivial, and/or what seems trivial to us), the things we cannot understand or are not ready to accept and take responsibility for, what makes us feel guilty or angry, and the embarrassing.

3. Answers will vary. Students should note that forgetting is related to the loss of civilization and values and identity, as well as lack of responsibility and maturity.

4. Answers will vary. Students should mention the connection of memory to education, responsibility, maturity, identity, and values.

5. Answers will vary. Students should mention that writing helps preserve memories; that writing can lead people to rely on the written word so that they don't exercise their minds; that oral societies preserve memories and educate through stories, poems, and public retellings; that the loss of writing contributes to the boys feeling out of their element without understanding why; that the first concrete result is no roll call. Students may conjecture that with a roll call, the older boys might have counted off and taken responsibility for groups of littluns and prevented the initial tragedy of the death of the boy with the birthmark. Students may think that the lack of a tool to help them schedule and plan contributed to the sense of a "play" existence, and thus to irresponsibility and action taken without heed for consequences.

Reality and Responsibility, page 84

1. Answers will vary. One important difference is the consequences of the choices made in the world of play and the real world.

2. Answers will vary. Students may connect responsibility to maturity and the concept of giving care to others who need assistance if and when they really need it, in the appropriate manner and to the appropriate extent. Students may think that responsibility is recognized through being assigned to it, finding one has a gift for doing it (whatever *it* is), or being in a relationship in which it is expected.

3. Possible responses: Jack's humiliated exclamation, "I'm not going to play any longer. Not with you," can be seen as a rejection of democracy, order, and responsibility; as a threat to the community led by Ralph; and as a choice for a life of moment-by-moment satiation of the senses. When Ralph appeals to Jack and the other "savages," saying, "You aren't playing the game—" he is appealing to their recollection of and acceptance of the shared principles of behavior that they had learned at home. His appeal is ironic because they no longer choose to acknowledge the customs and standards of civility and fairness as having any hold on them. When the officer says in response to Ralph's acknowledgment that there was no adult on the island, "Fun and games," he is suggesting that what has happened to them is in the realm of play, of trivial make-believe, of action without consequence. Given the reality of what had happened, his characterization is ironic and highlights the failure of adults to see the consequences of war in children's lives.

4. Students should note that Piggy recalls and tries to imitate the behavior of adults; that Jack and Roger (and, to a lesser degree, the other savages) celebrate the lack of constraint that exists without adults; and Ralph begins by focusing on trying to return to the world of adults, and sometimes slides into a fantasy world in which he imagines he is at home; Simon sees beyond the "wisdom" of adults who engage in wars to the heart of reality and meaning.

5. While acknowledging that there is no concerted effort, students should mention that Piggy tries to gather names and count littluns; Ralph leads the others in trying to build shelters and attempts to quell their fears; Simon helps them get food. They fail in personal care, in the example of behavior they set, in civility (as when Roger throws stones, pages 66–67), etc.

6. Students should discuss the role of avoidance, of euphemism, and of lies in dealing with the deaths, while noting the characters who remember and name the dead, and have the courage to recognize murder as such and name it.

7. Students should mention rites such as funerals, memorial services, viewing the body, wakes, graveside services, as well as counseling and support from peers and adults. The kind of deaths that occurred on the island could have brought charges of manslaughter and murder, with trial and imprisonment following. Students may think that the island society is not sophisticated and ordered enough for a court of justice. Some students may see Roger as being judge and executioner in a kind of parody of justice.

8. Students may mention courts, prison, probation and other facets of our criminal justice system; religious rites such as Reconciliation in the Catholic Church or Yom Kippur, the Jewish Day of Atonement; and psychological counseling, including behavior modification. Answers about consequences will vary. Golding's answer would seem to be "no" (see quotation in Question 9).

9. Students' answers should take account of the revelation the Lord of the Flies makes to Simon, as well as the goodness in Simon, who dies trying to remove his companions' supernatural fear of a natural object and the dedication of Piggy to the good of the group at his own expense. Students may agree or disagree with Golding's view, based on their understanding of human nature.

Fear, page 85

1. Answers will vary. Students may think that it is difficult to respond to fear of something that cannot be quantified, so the fear may become pervasive and hard to manage. Fear of what is known, when it is horrible, can also be consuming. Some students may recognize that fear of known things can have an unknown factor in it, for example, we all know we will die, but not exactly when and how; even if we know when and how we will meet something we fear, we don't know how we will bear it.

2. Answers will vary. Suggestions may include: facing what you fear; educating yourself; avoiding the feared thing.

3. Students may mention fears based in reality as including Piggy's fear of blindness; Ralph's fear of not being rescued; Ralph's fear that Jack and the savages will kill and behead him; Simon's fear of the nature of humanity as revealed by the Lord of the Flies. Fears from imaginary dangers include the fear of the "beast" as an external reality.

4. Students should give examples of how characters were motivated by fear, and how Jack used fear of "the beast" as a control and refused to let it die after Simon's death. They may also focus on the statement by the narrator on page 232, "[Ralph] forgot his wounds, his hunger and thirst, and became fear; hopeless fear on flying feet, rushing through the forest toward the open beach. . . ."

5. Answers will vary. Students may say in response to Boileau-Despréaux that fear of the beast was one of the things that led the boys into murder. In response to Gide, they may talk about the fear of the beast as embodied by the decaying body of the paratrooper and the sow's head. In response to Lerner, they may say that a true recognition of the "beast within" would have been the appropriate response—not facing the beast by externalizing it was a serious problem. In response to Nehru, they may site the description of the attack on Simon.

6. Students will probably say that in Golding's view, the corruption of people's hearts was the most fearful thing on the island. They may agree or disagree, depending on their assessment of human nature.

English Series

The Straight Forward English Series

is designed to measure, teach, review, and master specified English skills: capitalization and punctuation; nouns and pronouns; verbs; adjectives and adverbs; prepositions, conjunctions and interjections; sentences; clauses and phrases, and mechanics.

Each workbook is a simple, straightforward approach to learning English skills. Skills are keyed to major school textbook adoptions.

Pages are reproducible.

GP-032   **Capitalization and Punctuation**
GP-033   **Nouns and Pronouns**
GP-034   **Verbs**
GP-035   **Adjectives and Adverbs**
GP-041   **Sentences**
GP-043   **Prepositions, conjunctions, & Interjections**

Advanced Series

Large editions

GP-055   **Clauses & Phrases**
GP-056   **Mechanics**
GP-075   **Grammar & Diagramming Sentences**

Discovering Literature Series

The Discovering Literature Series

is designed to develop an appreciation for literature and to improve reading skills. Each guide in the series features an award winning novel and explores a wide range of critical reading skills and literature elements.

GP-076   **A Teaching Guide to My Side of the Mountain**
GP-077   **A Teaching Guide to Where the Red Fern Grows**
GP-078   **A Teaching Guide to Mrs. Frisby & the Rats of NIMH**
GP-079   **A Teaching Guide to Island of the Blue Dolphins**
GP-093   **A Teaching Guide to the Outsiders**
GP-094   **A Teaching Guide to Roll of Thunder**

Challenging Level

GP-090   **The Hobbit: A Teaching Guide**
GP-091   **Redwall: A Teaching Guide**
GP-092   **The Odyssey: A Teaching Guide**
GP-097   **The Giver: A Teaching Guide**
GP-096   **Lord of the Flies: A Teaching Guide**
GP-074   **To Kill A Mockingbird: A Teaching Guide**